BUILDING AMERICA
THEN AND NOW

THE NEW YORK CITY
SUBWAY SYSTEM

BUILDING AMERICA: THEN AND NOW

BUILDING AMERICA
THEN ᴀɴᴅ NOW

⫸ THE NEW YORK CITY ⫷
SUBWAY SYSTEM

RONALD A. REIS

CHELSEA HOUSE
PUBLISHERS
An imprint of Infobase Publishing

The New York City Subway System

Copyright © 2009 by Infobase Publishing

Chelsea House
An imprint of Infobase Publishing
132 West 31st Street
New York, NY 10001

Library of Congress Cataloging-in-Publication Data
Reis, Ronald A.
 The New York City subway system / by Ronald A. Reis.
   p. cm. — (Building America : then and now)
 Includes bibliographical references and index.
 ISBN 978-1-60413-046-1 (hardcover)
 1. Subways—New York (State)—New York—History—Juvenile literature. 2. New York (New York)—Transportation—History—Juvenile literature. 3. Urban transportation—United States—History—Juvenile literature. I. Title. II. Series.

 TF847.N5R45 2009
 388.4'28097471—dc22   2008025550

Chelsea House books are available at special discounts when purchased in bulk quantities for businesses, associations, institutions, or sales promotions. Please call our Special Sales Department in New York at (212) 967-8800 or (800) 322-8755.

You can find Chelsea House on the World Wide Web at http://www.chelseahouse.com

Text design by Annie O'Donnell
Cover design by Ben Peterson

Printed in the United States of America

Bang NMSG 10 9 8 7 6 5 4 3 2 1

This book is printed on acid-free paper.

All links and Web addresses were checked and verified to be correct at the time of publication. Because of the dynamic nature of the Web, some addresses and links may have changed since publication and may no longer be valid.

CONTENTS

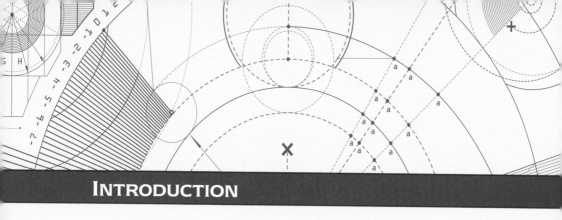

Secret Subway

In 1912, workers digging to create the Broadway Subway, north of Murray Street in lower Manhattan, hit a brick wall approximately 21 feet (6.4 meters) below the street surface. Breaking through the wall, the laborers came upon a tunnel 9 feet (2.7 m) in diameter and lined with eight-inch-thick (20.32 centimeters) bricks. Two rails led into a midnight void, which, it would turn out, curved abruptly at 90 degrees, extending approximately 300 feet (91.44 m) to beneath Park Place. Most startling of all, the excavators, groping forward with shovels in hand, soon came upon the remains of a wooden car—a subway car. Obviously, someone had, a long time earlier, attempted to do what was now being done: build a subterranean transport system. The New York Subway of 1912 was, unmistakably, not the first to be dug beneath the city. Someone—at least on an experimental basis—had been there, done that, before.

That someone was Alfred Ely Beach, publisher of *Scientific American* magazine. In 1868, he had begun to dig a tube through which he hoped to fit a subway car that would be propelled forward and backward by air pressure. "A tube, a car, and a revolving fan," the young inventor was to declare, was all it would take to relieve late nineteenth-century New Yorkers of massive gridlock above ground. The 22-passenger car that Beach would create for his Beach Pneumatic Transit Company was to "shoot" commuters through the tunnel like a projectile.

Such systems had been built before, to carry mail and packages. In 1859, in London, England, pneumatically propelled cars, which ran underground on rails in large pipes, connected the London Post Office with the Charing Cross Railway Station. On the inaugural run, several men lay down in the cars and were whisked through the tubes along with the mail. If the system were enlarged, Beach speculated, why couldn't passengers be carried—not on their backs, but sitting up in style and comfort?

In 1867, Beach tested his plan above ground. During the American Institute Fair, at New York's 14th Street Armory, the inventor suspended a 107-foot-long (32.6 m) tube, 6 feet (1.8 m) in diameter, from the ceiling. A 10-passenger car was driven inside the tube—first in one direction by suction, and then in the opposite direction by a blast of air. An ordinary 8-blade, 10-foot-diameter (3.04 m) fan, spinning at 250 revolutions per minute and driven by a 15-horsepower steam engine, gave more than 75,000 fairgoers the ride of a lifetime. Beach was awarded the Gold Medal of the American Institute for his novel transport system.

A year later, the publisher began to dig. He had received a permit to build a pneumatic package delivery system, which consisted of two small tunnels to be dug from Warren Street to Cedar Street. Failing to receive authorization to build what he really wanted—a full-fledged passenger subway—Beach had to settle for mail tubes. The inventor began to dig a single large tunnel, to later be divided (he assured city officials) into two separate, smaller mail-carrying tubes. In actuality, Beach was digging for a different purpose; his eight-man crew took out far more soil than would be necessary for the mere transport of mail and packages.

Beach and his crew were building a subway. According to Brian J. Cudahy, author of *Under the Sidewalks of New York*:

> Beach's construction crews worked in the dead of night and began their tunnel through the *basement* of Devlin's clothing store on Broadway at Murray Street. Dirt from the bore was smuggled out through the store in a manner not unlike that associated with the digging of escape tunnels in World War II prisoner-of-war movies.

Built by Alfred Beach, an inventor and publisher of *Scientific American*, the pneumatic subway was designed to transport passengers by using air pressure to push the cars to and from their destinations. After New York City officials shut it down, the pneumatic subway *(above)* became a forgotten form of underground transportation.

On February 26, 1870, Alfred Ely Beach opened his $350,000 pneumatic subway to an eager and curious New York. According to the *New York Times*, in an article published the following day:

> Yesterday the tunnel was thrown open to the inspection of visitors for the first time, and it must be said that every one of them came away surprised and gratified. Such as expected to find a dismal, cavernous retreat under Broadway, opened their eyes at the elegant reception room, the light, airy tunnel and the general appearance of taste and comfort in all the apartments, and those who entered to pick out some scientific flaw in the project, were silenced by the completeness of the machinery, the solidity of the work, and the safety of the running apparatus.

In the subway's first year of operation, 400,000 New Yorkers paid 25 cents apiece to enjoy a football-field-long ride. They were transported from one end to the other, between Warren and Murray streets. By all accounts, it was a thrilling yet serene 10-mile-per-hour (16 kilometers per hour) jaunt.

Such excursions were not to last, however. In 1873, the Beach Demonstration Tunnel was closed and sealed up. Finance and politics, it was said, were to blame. Soon enough, out of sight became out of mind. New York would forget its first attempt to burrow a subway, limited as it was.

Thirty years passed before the city again dug a subway of a different sort. Out in the open—literally and figuratively—the Interborough Rapid Transit (IRT) system would eventually become the largest, most complex public rapid-transit system in the world. During its early construction, New Yorkers would be reminded that an inventor of singular importance—one Alfred Ely Beach—was looking ahead long before, anticipating what was to come.

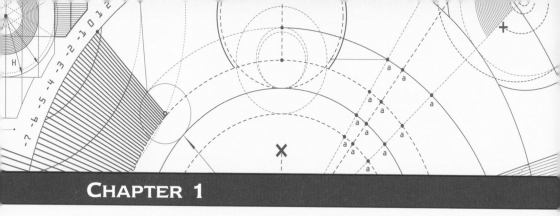

CHAPTER 1

City Streets

When the Civil War ended in 1865, New York City exploded. Not from bombs and munitions, although the city had seen its share of turmoil in the previous four years, particularly as a result of the draft riots of 1863. New York's postwar boom was not in armaments, however—it was in people.

Manhattan Island—23 square miles (59.5 sq km) of rock located in an upper Atlantic bay—would soon experience a massive, unprecedented influx from all over the world, particularly Europe. From 1865 to 1900, its population leaped fivefold, from 700,000 to 3.5 million. Parts of Manhattan, most notably the Lower East Side, achieved population densities greater than any other place on Earth. There was no doubt about it: In the last half of the nineteenth century, New York City was *the* place to be.

As a consequence, getting around the city—specifically the commercially vibrant southern tip of Manhattan, below 14th Street—was becoming almost hopeless. Light industry and retailing competed with the financial business of Wall Street to create an island alive with activity—working, shopping, sightseeing, and just living. Getting from one place to another, be it on foot or by carriage, was not only a drawn-out, obstacle-prone affair, it was also a dangerous one. "Omnibuses, horsecars, hansom cabs, carriages, and drays raced up and down eighty-foot-wide Broadway, all unfettered by traffic lights," reported Lorraine Diehl in *Subways: The Tracks That Built New York City.* "Pedestrians didn't stand a chance." A *New York Tribune* writer declared, "We can travel from New York half-way to Philadelphia in less time than the length of Broadway."

Until the late 1880s, the various forms of street transport used to move people across town and uptown were all propelled by horses. The animals themselves presented their own problems, including environmental damage, which made life in the city not only depressing but also—according to some—life threatening.

Horse manure and urine were the main problems, and disposing of 15,000 carcasses each year added to city woes. The average urban horse dropped, often "in route," 22 pounds (10 kilograms) of dung a day, plus a quart of urine. With no less than 120,000 horses in Manhattan by century's end, a great deal of animal waste was created, much of which had to be wallowed through by disgusted pedestrians. In 1890, 22,000 "depositing" horses and mules were required simply to pull streetcars through New York City and Brooklyn.

Citizens constantly complained of "pulverized horse dung" blowing in their faces. The paving of streets only made matters worse, as hoofs and wheels ground the manure against the hard surfaces and increased dust particles. In 1908, Harold Bolce—writing in *Appleton's Magazine*—charged that, each year, 20,000 New Yorkers died from "maladies that fly in the dust, created mainly by horse manure."

In addition to fraying people's nerves and sullying the environment, the congestion had serious negative economic consequences. "Merchants warned that the city faced an economic crisis as the cost of moving goods through congested streets forced business to depart," declared Michael Brooks in *Subway*

City: Riding the Trains, Reading New York. "The tax base would shrink and rents would soar in congested residential quarters." It was clear, as a *New York Times* article predicted in 1873, that "New York would soon become a city of the very rich and the very poor, of those who can afford to stay and those who cannot leave."

DOWNTOWN MISERY/UPTOWN UTOPIA

Overcrowding was most acute on Manhattan's East Side. Particularly crowded was the Lower East Side, which spread north and south from Delancey Street. As many as 9,000 residents per acre were crammed into airless, wooden, fire-prone tenement houses, apartments where there was no running water and individuals had to use street "island" privies to relieve themselves, often in the cold dead of night.

These tenement houses were "dark, airless apartments so crowded you couldn't turn around," reported Vivian Heller in *The City Beneath Us: Building the New York Subways.* "No light, no air, no privacy, no space—this was the New York that countless immigrants knew, a city strangled by its own growth."

The Lower East Side was an ethnic enclave of hardworking immigrants, primarily eastern European Jews who took up residency in the 1880s and 1890s. Many based their livelihoods on the burgeoning New York garment industry. In one year alone, 1892, a half million immigrants passed through Ellis Island, their portal of entry. Most of them stayed in New York City.

Life in the East Side slums was, more often than not, pure torment. "Wherever you turned, you were confronted with garbage and filth," Vivian Heller explained. "Cholera, typhus, tuberculosis, yellow fever—these were the daily companions of the poor." "Air, give me air!" was the ever-present cry from those trapped in such suffocating conditions with little hope of escape.

It is no wonder, then, that many of the city's poverty-stricken residents turned to radical politics in an attempt to elevate their plight. "Socialists and anarchists were multiplying on the Lower

By 1855, there were 593 giant stagecoaches on 27 routes and 4 separate railways operating in bustling New York City, all of which used horses that left layers of filth and grime on the streets. The city's roads were so clogged with people, horses, and vehicles that many pedestrians gave up trying to walk on them.

East Side, captivating huge audiences," Vivian Heller stated. "Fear began to spread into the gilded salons of the rich: the fear of revolution: the fear of disease—there was always the specter of an epidemic, a plague engulfing the city."

New York mayor Abram Hewitt, who entered office in 1887, took up the cry for relief—but not as a champion of the downtrodden. On the contrary, his main purpose in seeking a remedy for the poor of the Lower East Side, Little Italy, and Hell's

Kitchen was to get "undesirables" out of town and away from Manhattan.

"To the mind and spirit of the city's capitalist Puritans who enthusiastically supported Hewitt, the working class's collective love for all things loose and leisurely was not only wasteful, tasteless, and ungodly, but, they quickly learned, unstoppable," reported Marc Eliot in *Down 42nd Street*. "To get rid of the daily flow of immigrants into the city, Hewitt devised a plan to ship them off every evening en masse to the raw Siberia of the outer boroughs, where he insisted they belonged and hoped they would stay."

Moving from downtown misery to uptown utopia would not be easy, no matter who took the ride. Yet the goal was now clear, the vision unobstructed. All agreed that the living and working conditions in lower Manhattan had become untenable. A way would have to be found to get people uptown—maybe even as far as the outer boroughs—to live, and then get them back south to work. Clearly, the city's horsecars, streetcars, and omnibuses could not do the job. Street traffic was simply too strangled and obstructed. A plan was needed to lift commuters above the fray, to travel swiftly on some sort of elevated railway. There would be no shortage of schemes claiming they could do just that.

SCHEMING AND DREAMING

Early proposals for elevated railroads—where tracks would be supported above streets or sidewalks by columns—began to appear as early as the 1840s. By 1867, as if it wanted to cover all angles, the New York State legislature actually debated plans for a three-tier road. It would, according to the *New York Times*, be a multilevel structure consisting of steam-powered elevated trains above, horsecars on the street, and subway tracks for freight deliveries below. It never happened.

By 1873, Simeon Church, a crusader for rapid transit, declared (as quoted by Michael Brooks), "All manner of schemes, underground, overground, three-tier, viaduct, depressed, arcade, marginal, tube, tunnel, and what not have been pressed with all manner of pictures, plates, models, drawings, and designs endorsed by imposing certificates, bearing imposing and illustrious names. . . . We stand today with absolutely nothing done."

One of the most ingenious designs for an elevated railway, or "el," came from Alfred Speer. In Speer's scheme, the train itself was absent. What the inventor proposed was nothing less

BUILDING AMERICA NOW

MASSACHUSETTS BAY TRANSPORTATION AUTHORITY (MBTA)

Boston, the birthplace of the nation's liberty, is also the birthplace of America's mass transit. The city, which found itself in a similar situation to New York at the end of the nineteenth century—that is, overcrowded and facing an enormous strain on traffic in the commercial downtown area—was desperate for some type of rapid-transit relief. The first electric streetcar line, in the city's hub, began operation on January 1, 1889. Today's Green Line/Beacon Street route was part of this first installation. On September 1, 1897, the Boston Transit Commission funded the excavation and construction of America's first subway, nicknamed the "T."

An interesting feature of today's MBTA is the transit-oriented development (TOD) project, in which compact, walkable development around transit stations is encouraged. The idea is to include a mix of uses such as housing, shopping, employment, and recreational facilities. According to the MBTA Web site (http://mbta.com), "TOD represents an opportunity for communities all across Massachusetts to enhance their quality of life by turning parking lots and underutilized land near public transportation into vibrant mixed-use districts, diverse housing, and lively public places."

than a giant conveyance: a conveyor belt–driven promenade, a horizontal escalator. Essentially, Speer's Endless Railway Train, as it was called, would consist of a city-long platform carried on friction wheels and powered by below-ground engines. The belt would move up and down Broadway at 10 to 12 miles (16 to 19 km) per hour. According to Brooks, "Pedestrians could stroll and show off their clothes. A gentleman could ride in a smoking compartment. Ladies could repair to toilet rooms provided with female attendants. Or they could stand at the rail, watching the city move past. New Yorkers in a hurry could walk. Their legs and the moving platform would reach a combined speed of 16 miles per hour." In other words, Speer was proposing a huge, intricate "people mover" with added luxuries.

On a smaller scale was Charles T. Harvey's plan for a "one-legged railway," so called because it consisted of a single, slender track running above a sidewalk. The track was supported by 30-foot-high (9.1 m) columns. According to Lorraine Diehl, "On a cold Sunday morning in December 1867, Charles Harvey made a special trial run just for supporters of his elevated, taking a quarter-mile ride from the Battery to Morris Street, riding high above the gawking spectators in his specially built handcar: a glorified go-cart with giant metal wheels." Unfortunately, at least for Harvey, his experiment in constructing a cable-driven elevated train ended when the financial panic of September 24, 1869, forced his company into bankruptcy.

Perhaps the most visionary plan of all—one that, in effect, incorporated subway elements—was proposed by Melville C. Smith in 1866. Smith would essentially build an upper and lower Broadway. In the developer's scheme, which was known as the Arcade Railway, there would be a dignified Broadway above, and a new, more utilitarian Broadway below. According to Brooks, "The advantage of the Arcade over all other possible schemes was that it would extend Broadway's historic functions as a street of travel, shopping, and fashionable strolling." Although Smith spent $500,000 on surveys and engineering studies, his plan never materialized. Smith's model of the project is now on display in the Museum of the City of New York.

Yet, New York would eventually have its els. Rapid transit, at least above ground, was to be a reality.

STEAMING ELS

The first Manhattan el to justifiably call itself such opened for business on February 14, 1870. Its three wooden cable-driven passenger cars ran from Dey Street to 30th Street on the West Side. The single-track elevated—which converted to steam

ELECTRIFICATION:
Power to Go

When the first IRT subway line opened in 1904, its trains were powered by what was then the largest steam-powered electrical generating power plant in the world. Each of 10 massive dynamos (generators) put out 11,000 volts of alternating current (AC) that was first sent to eight substations located throughout the subway route. There, transformers reduced the high voltage to 625 volts. Because the subway's train motors were designed to operate on direct current (DC), converters were used to rectify the AC to DC. From the converters, direct current was sent to two rails on the subway line: one the positive rail, the other the negative, or return, rail. The latter was designated the "third rail." One hundred years later, the basic method of supplying current to power New York's subway trains remains (with obvious expansion aside) unchanged.

According to the Web site How Stuff Works (http://www.howstuff works.com):

The third rail lies outside or between the subway tracks, and a wheel, brush, or sliding shoe carries the power from the rail to the train's electrical motor. [The power is returned via one of the power soon after—would eventually become the Ninth Avenue El, taking its place with three other such systems on Second, Third, and Sixth avenues. By 1880, Manhattan had four fully functional, steam-powered elevated trains running up and down the island. There were a total of 81 miles (130.3 km) of track "winding around the serpentine curve of the Lower East Side's Coenties Slip and stretching high over the daunting Suicide Curve at 110th Street," as noted by Lorraine Diehl.

The steam engines that pulled the wooden cars of the early els were "minis," or diminutive steam locomotives. Both the

two running rails.] In the New York City subway system, the third rail carries 625 volts of electricity, and the original lines required their own power plant to operate. A series of cables and substations carried the electricity from the power plant to the third rail.

Of course, power to the rails is one thing; power to operate the subway's signals, ventilation, line equipment, and station and tunnel lighting is another story altogether. Here, alternating current is used. Except for electronic equipment, no rectification to direct current is required. The two power systems—one for operating the trains, the other for everything else—are kept separate. That way, if one fails, the other is unaffected. Thus, if power to the third rail goes down and trains can't move, lighting is still available throughout the system. Conversely, if lighting fails, the trains can still proceed.

Power usage, of course, is determined by operational needs. At 8:30 A.M., the New York Subway system is at maximum capacity, drawing 100 percent of its electrical needs. Conversely, at 3:30 A.M., the subway system requires only 42 percent of what is provided at peak time.

engines and the cars were essentially scaled-down versions of regular railroad equipment. Their top speed on the elevated lines was 14 miles (22.5 km) per hour.

Clearly the els served their purpose of opening up suburban Manhattan to those downtown. Yet, although the els were seen as necessary by both patrons and residents, they eventually came to represent the grimier, harder edge of urban life in New York City. According to Marc Eliot, "Besides being unconnected to each other, slow, outmoded, under-routed, and overcrowded, the deafening overhead rail systems that lumbered along 50 feet above the street thrust the streets below them into the grinding screech and dreary gray of endless sunless days. It was estimated at one point that citizens living beneath or adjacent to the elevateds put up with as much as 19 hours of rumbling and roaring every day, seven days a week."

There was more. Doctors discovered that, at each station, elevated trains were grinding off small iron particles from their brake shoes. These metal shavings, bordered with jagged fringes, were getting into people's eyes.

Of course, traveling high above street level often gave riders the opportunity to do a little peeping into second- and third-story windows that the train passed by. The views could be fascinating. "The elevateds provided a direct view into the housing of the poor," Michael Brooks noted. "Look through any of the windows, which are all open, and you see . . . a supper table spread and the family seated around it. You will generally see a bed in the same room, for there is no place to spare."

At the station platforms, especially during rush hour, decorum was often lost. "Pushing, swaying, leaning forward to peer down the track, crowding past one another with the intention of getting to the points which they calculate will be opposite the car platforms when the train stops, they run the risk of being pushed upon the track at every moment," the *New York Tribune* reported in 1890.

Still, by the last decade of the nineteenth century, the els had, as Marc Eliot noted, "performed a key role in helping to bring Manhattan's population farther northward, which in turn helped speculators develop raw land into livable real estate, so much so that by the end of that year [1890], the average Manhattanite was clocking almost 300 mass transit trips a year."

Although el ridership was impressive, a decline in patronage was coming. The little steam engines that could were struggling to pull forward, and their technology for elevated use was rapidly running down. A new way to move trains over rails was needed to get the els "back on track" with passengers and the general public alike. The els would have to go electric, as the street railways beneath them had recently done.

ELECTRIFICATION OF THE RAILS

By the end of the nineteenth century, Manhattan's steam-puffing elevateds were, indeed, in trouble. Ridership had fallen from a high of 219 million in 1893 to 191.1 million in 1901. What was killing off the four els? The electrification of surface streetcars.

In 1890, just 15.5 percent of all surface conveyance was by electrical power. By 1902, the number had exploded to an astonishing 97 percent. That streetcar companies would take to electrification so quickly is hardly surprising, given electrical power's tremendous advantages over horsepower. When unhampered by street congestion, an electrical streetcar traveled three times faster than a horsecar, at a speed of seven miles per hour. As a result, streetcar companies were able to extend their lines uptown (and beyond) into undeveloped areas. Doing so stimulated residential development along the routes, which, in turn, increased streetcar patronage. Between 1890 and 1903, the total number of passengers riding on the electrically driven surface railways of Manhattan grew an astonishing 50 percent.

On the other hand, as has been noted, steam-powered elevated lines—although charming to some—were more than a

New York City's first elevated train ran along Ninth Avenue on the West Side. The steam-powered train was popular with the public and was soon joined by elevated train lines on Second, Third, and Sixth avenues. These trains, running almost three stories above the streets, allowed residents to travel, shop, and work in different parts of the city.

nuisance to most people. "The engines were sooty, messy, and noisy," Brian Cudahy declared. "They started fires in awnings, startled teams of horses, and in general wreaked havoc with efforts to lead a quiet and tranquil life."

To have electricity drive vehicles of any kind, however, particularly elevateds, the industry needed its own Thomas Edison—a person who could apply the "spark" to transportation as the famous inventor had done to light. They found such an individual in Frank Sprague.

In 1888, Sprague, in what is considered the first successful electric transportation installation, outfitted a 12-mile (19 km), 30-trolley car system for Richmond, Virginia, with electrical motors and an overhead wire system for power distribution. Yet, to produce an electrical schema that could propel elevateds and, eventually, subways, Sprague would need to take a giant leap forward. He had to carry his designs to a new level, figuratively and literally.

What the inventor came up with would be known as *multiple-unit control*, a technology that defined urban mass transit to come. According to Brian Cudahy, "Multi-unit control, as the name suggests, allows the motorman [locomotive engineer] in the lead car of a multi-car train to operate the motors of all cars from a single control station. . . . Sprague's pioneering work gave the transit industry the technology breakthrough that was desperately needed. Sprague's success meant that trains could be lengthened or shortened at will and as traffic warranted."

Multiple-unit control was just what the els needed. As Cudahy declared, "In short, multiple-unit control made the change from steam to electricity more than merely having electric locomotives haul the same cars previously hauled by the steam locomotives. Each car would now contain its own power unit, all efficiently controlled by a motorman in the lead car."

The Manhattan Railway Company, which operated the city's four els, lost no time in taking advantage of Sprague's pioneering creation. Three years after the switch to electricity began in 1901, the elevateds carried 50 percent more riders than before. Interestingly, though, surface transport did not suffer from the elevateds' new success. In 1898, the els carried 184 million passengers, while surface streetcars hauled 321 million. By 1903, the year before the city's first subway line opened, el ridership had shot up to 246 million, thanks to electrification. The surface cars, however, took an even greater share of total passengers: 427 million.

By century's end, it had become clear: New York City, with its 3.5 million residents, needed all the rapid transit it could get—on the surface, above ground, and, if possible, below the streets. New York City needed a subway!

CHAPTER 2

An Audacious Plan

At century's end, New York City was desperate to expand what little rapid transit it had. The reason was obvious: The city itself was expanding geographically. Prior to 1898, New York City was the island of Manhattan—essentially 2 miles (3.2 km) by 13 miles (20.9 km) in Upper New York Bay. In 1898, as a result of city unification, New York increased from 24 (62 sq km) to 322 square miles (834 sq km). Most of the additionally acquired land was either undeveloped or consisted of small farming communities. As a new, enlarged city—the City of Greater New York—the potential for enormous growth was at hand. One new territory in particular had already developed into a thriving metropolis, second only to Manhattan itself.

With unification, New York City became five boroughs, or political divisions. North of what is now the borough of Manhattan, across the 750-foot-wide (228.6 m) Harlem River, lay the 44-square-mile (114 sq km) Bronx borough. To the south, in Lower New York Bay, were the 60 square miles (155.3 sq km) of the Staten Island borough. To the east, across the East River, at the western extension of Long Island, were the boroughs of Queens (112 square miles [290 sq km]) and Brooklyn (82 square miles [212.3 sq km])—the former to the north, the latter to the south. Of the four new boroughs beyond Manhattan, Brooklyn was clearly the more developed; the northeastern end had incorporated as a city in 1834.

According to Michelle Stacey, author of the cultural history *The Fasting Girl: A True Victorian Medical Mystery*:

> Brooklyn could, by 1860, boast a massive shipbuilding industry based at the Brooklyn Navy Yard; its own railroads, ferries, and horsecar lines; numerous manufacturing businesses (including the largest hat-making company in the country); and a substantial chip on its shoulder about being a city in its own right rather than merely a smaller, less impressive cousin to Manhattan.

So consequential was Brooklyn, even before city unification, and so desirous was it for people either working or living there to cross into Manhattan, that in 1883 a momentous project was completed: the Brooklyn Bridge. The bridge, which spanned the East River, was desperately needed to relieve the already overburdened ferries that had traveled the salty waters since Robert Fulton began service in 1814.

Brooklyn even had its own railroad, its own rapid transit of sorts. Most of the lines, known as excursion railways, went south from the city proper to the developing beach resorts at Brighton Beach and Coney Island. One development activity fed the other. With more steam-powered trains traveling to the beaches, more hotels and resorts could be built; the latter, in turn, demanded more and better transport. Referring to the inaugural run of the Brighton Beach line in 1878, the *Brooklyn Eagle* declared, "The big engine . . . puffed and snorted at the station . . . as if impatient to start away on the wings of the wind. The initial portion of the trip was through tunnels and cuts 50 feet deep from which nothing but the sky was visible."

Soon enough, Brooklyn boasted its very own el. Known as the Kings County Elevated, it linked up with the Brighton Beach Line in 1896 to form a basic, everyday mass-transit service. In the same year, the Brooklyn Rapid Transit Company (BRT) was formed. Three years later, the company did away with steam locomotives and converted its line to electric power. Then, in 1899, the BRT made arrangements to operate its elevated trains across the Brooklyn Bridge to Manhattan. Everyone on both sides of the East River knew that such a link would never be enough. In short order, river crossers began to talk about additional bridges and even a subway. If the latter were to be built, however, it would have to travel under the 2,000-foot-wide (609.6 m) river itself.

MAPPING IT OUT

Alfred Ely Beach's pneumatic experiment aside, real nineteenth-century subways did exist. The world's first passenger-carrying urban system to operate beneath the surface—the "Underground"—was the 3.7-mile (6 km) track in London that opened on January 10, 1863. By 1900, three additional European cities, Glasgow, Budapest, and Paris, had subways under construction. Boston, after three years of digging, opened America's first subway in 1898 (limited as it was).

The first serious proposal to do likewise in New York, though on a much grander scale, came from Mayor Abram Hewitt on January 31, 1888. This is the same mayor, as has been noted, who was searching for a way to get "undesirables" (Italians, Russians, and Austrian-Hungarians) off the island of Manhattan. However, Hewitt also wanted to retain middle-class and skilled working-class folks, lest they flee to Brooklyn and New Jersey, taking their tax dollars with them. A rapid-transit subway that would open the northern reaches of Manhattan (and perhaps travel into the Bronx) was just what was needed.

In putting forth his proposal, Hewitt suggested a method of financing that was untried before, at least in the United States. He wanted the municipal government to finance the line and a

The expansion of New York City necessitated accessible transport from the boroughs to Manhattan. Like Budapest, London, and Boston, New York City's solution was an underground transit system. *Above,* laborers rip out streets to allow for the construction of subway tunnels.

private company to build and manage it. Previously, all transit lines of any consequence were strictly private affairs. Hewitt felt the government needed to be involved, however, both as a civic responsibility and to ward off corruption.

It took the "Blizzard of 1888," which completely immobilized New York City and shut down every type of transit line, to reveal how important transportation was to a large, tightly confined urban area. According to Clifton Hood, author of *772 Miles: The Building of the Subways and How They Transformed New York*:

> For two days that March snow swept out of New Jersey and across the Hudson, propelled by winds that reached fifty miles per hour. Mountains of snow 20 to 25 feet high covered street lamps and brownstone stoops, reaching the second floor of some buildings. With gale force winds reducing visibility to less

than half a foot, many pedestrians were blown off their feet and had to crawl on their hands and knees. Some did not make it to safety and froze to death in the streets.

The Hewitt formula to finance rapid transit—a public/private partnership—failed to impress free-market city elders at the time. Yet the desirability of a subway, where trains would travel 40 to 50 miles (64.3 to 80.4 km) per hour beneath the city, more or less unaffected by weather conditions on the surface, had gained acceptance.

In 1891, development toward the subway goal moved a step forward with the formation of the Steinway Commission. This commission, though still wedded to the proposition that any subway enterprise would have to be a private undertaking, came up with a planned subway route that would run from South Ferry at Manhattan's southern tip to the Bronx. Yet in December 1892, when the commission tried to auction off rights to a private firm to build the subway, it came up empty; not one serious bid emerged. Banks were not prepared to take the risk and loan money ($50 to $100 million) to a private firm that wanted to undertake such a task.

Finally, with passage of New York State's Rapid Transit Act of 1894, the idea of a municipally constructed subway system that would, in turn, be leased to private interests for operation under a long-term contract took hold. What emerged in the next couple of years was a plan similar to what the Steinway Commission had proposed, but with public, not private, financing. With the formation of Greater New York City in 1898, subway construction was all but assured.

THE CONTRACT

The final subway route would be a compromise, to keep the cost below the $50 million required by law. Still, it would represent a massive undertaking—one that would open up new land for development in upper Manhattan and beyond. According to Clifton Hood, the route for what would be known as Contract One,

> would go up the east side from city hall to Grand Central Terminal, then across Forty-second Street to Longacre Square (now Times Square) on the west side, and then up Broadway to Ninety-sixth Street, where it would divide into two branches, with one branch following Broadway through Harlem, Washington Heights, Fort George, and Riverdale in what is now the Bronx, and the other branch running up Lenox Avenue, across the Harlem River, and going to Bronx Park.

On November 13, 1899, the Rapid Transit Commission opened the bidding for a franchise to build the subway. On January 16, 1900, it awarded the $35 million contract to the lowest bidder, John B. McDonald, an experienced builder of railroad tunnels and a man with solid political connections to Tammany Hall.

McDonald had quit school at an early age to help support his family. Nonetheless, he rose rapidly in the growing field of construction management. A man who possessed much physical strength in his short, stocky body, he was, according to the *Morning Journal*, "a picture of resolute strength and splendid energy."

McDonald was a builder who knew how to manage his labor and how to finish a job on time and within budget. He was also a person with extreme confidence. On receiving the contract to build New York's first subway, the 54-year-old McDonald told the *World*, "Why there is nothing to this job—but hard work. I tell you it is simply a case of cellar digging on a grand scale. Just take all the cellars in the city and string 'em together." As the proud McDonald would find out soon enough, however, there was a lot more to building a subway than stretching cellars one after the other.

Although McDonald had abundant confidence, he lacked money. He did not have enough to cover the $7 million bond necessary to reimburse the city, in case he was unable to complete the work. Enter wealthy banker August Belmont, a man who had plenty of money and was always looking for, as quoted by Clifton Hood, "the splendid opportunities . . . for making a great deal of

PATH:
Another River to Cross

While engineers and construction crews were busy building a suspension bridge across the East River (the Brooklyn Bridge) in the last half of the nineteenth century, to link Manhattan Island with Brooklyn, attempts to span the Hudson River were also proceeding by tunneling down under. Begun in 1874 by a railroad engineer named DeWitt Clinton Haskin, the ambitious plan called for a pair of single-track tunnels to be dug from Jersey City, New Jersey, to a large union station that would be built under Washington Square in Greenwich Village. Haskin was able to complete about 40 percent of the 4,800-foot-long (1,463 m) tunnel before it became apparent that the technology of the day would not allow him to proceed. Attempts to resume excavation and digging of the same tunnel took place in 1890 but were again stopped, this time for financial reasons.

A third attempt was made to finish tunnel construction in 1902, via a new construction method that used tubular cast-iron plating to reinforce tunnel walls. Finally, in 1907, the first trains began to run, under the ownership of the Hudson and Manhattan Railroad formed by enterprising entrepreneur William G. McAdoo. By 1911, the initial project to link New Jersey with Manhattan by train was considered complete, at a cost of $60 million.

Today, the tunnels that McAdoo built (and other cross-river transport) are run by the Port Authority Trans-Hudson Corporation (PATH), a subsidiary of the Port Authority of New York and New Jersey. The PATH's World Trade Center station was destroyed in the terrorist attacks of September 11, 2001. A temporarily restored station, which cost $323 million, opened at the site on November 23, 2003. A permanent station, expected to cost a whopping $3.2 billion, is scheduled for completion by 2013.

money out of schemes for improving the transportation of our large and growing cities."

When McDonald approached Belmont, the financier quickly agreed to come up with the $7 million. Belmont then formed the Rapid Transit Subway Construction Company that would build the subway. Soon after, he created the Interborough Rapid Transit Company that would operate it. Thus, the deal was set, summarized as follows by Clifton Hood:

> On February 21, 1900, Belmont signed a contract, known as Contract No. 1, to build, equip, and operate the railway for a period of 50 years and renewable for another 25 years. The municipal government agreed to give Belmont $35 million to cover the cost of construction, plus $1.5 million to buy land for the stations and terminals. In return, Belmont agreed to supply the cars, signals, and other equipment out of his own pocket. When the subway opened, Belmont would pay an annual rental equal to the interest on the construction bond, plus a small sum for a sinking fund.

The city would own the subway, but it would be built and run by Belmont's companies. In essence, financier Belmont now ran the show. He would hire McDonald to do the actual subway construction, but he would first have to find someone to design the system.

THE JOB AT HAND

That man, it turned out, was William Barclay Parsons, already on hand as chief engineer for the recently formed Rapid Transit Commission of 1894. Parsons, born in 1859, spent his early years acquiring an education in England. He remained an admirer of everything British, particularly its aristocratic upper class.

In 1875, Parsons enrolled at Columbia College. According to Clifton Hood, "He was a big, strapping youth who was good at games and was popular with his classmates despite a humorless streak that earned him the unattractive nickname, 'Reverend

Parsons.' " Parsons graduated from Columbia in 1879 and, three years later, received a degree in civil engineering from the university's School of Mines.

Soon enough, Parsons worked his way up the ladder of his profession, gaining ever more challenging assignments with various firms in the New York City area. As early as 1890, he became fascinated with the possibility of rapid transit, particularly the subway. As Clifton Hood described, "He pored over topographical maps of Manhattan and hiked through city neighborhoods trying to figure out the best route, motive power, and construction methods for an underground railway."

A man known to exhibit little personal warmth yet remain calm under pressure (with rigid self-control), Parsons drew first-rate engineers to his side. The engineer saw the subway he was about to design as a mission rather than a mere job. Yet the building of New York City's first subway line through bustling Manhattan would certainly not be easy.

Though they were not Parsons's direct concern, there would, for starters, be legal issues surrounding the building of a subway in a metropolitan area where not all of the residents agreed with the plan. Some property owners were more than willing to claim all manner of damages that construction of such a subway might inflict on them. What occurred during the building of the city's elevateds in this regard did not bode well for the subway. According to an article written in 1904 (the year the subway opened) that appears on the New York Subway Web site:

> The experience of the elevated railroad corporations in building their lines had shown the uncertainty of depending upon legal precedents. It was not, at that time, supposed that the abutting property owners would have any legal ground for complaint against the elevated structures, but the courts found new laws for new conditions and spelled out new property rights of light, air, and access, which were made the basis of a volume of litigation unprecedented in the courts of any country.

Steps would have to be taken to ensure that costly lawsuits did not hamper subway construction. Ultimately (and under multiple contracts), the job consisted of building 21 miles (33.7 km) of tunnels and 58 miles (93.3 km) of tracks (not to be confused with route miles). Of those, 46.5 miles (74.8 km) would be built underground and 11.5 miles (18.5 km) along elevated lines. There would be 43 local stations, 5 express stations, and 10 station elevators. The project was to be completed in four and a half years. With Parsons picking up a ceremonial pickax and thrust-

William Parsons, the chief engineer of the New York City Subway, decided to avoid the potential problems and complications involved with digging deep tunnels for the transit system, opting instead for a shallow excavation. After laborers created a large trench in a city street, they set up wooden crossbeams (*above*) to lay across a temporary steel bed above their work site.

ing it into the ground on March 24, 1900, actual construction of the New York Subway system began.

BETWEEN A ROCK AND A HARD PLACE

Unfortunately, it would take thousands of pickaxes, wielded by thousands of laborers, to break up the streets and rocks of Manhattan Island. Very little powered construction equipment, such as steam shovels and bulldozers, was available to diggers in 1900. It would be hard work, done by hand, and it would take at its peak 2,700 men—a good many of them immigrants—to dig and construct the New York Subway system's initial route.

To begin with, Parsons had to decide how he was going to deal with Manhattan's 450-million-year-old metamorphic bed-rock known as *schist*. There were two concentrations of the mica-based rock near enough to the surface to cause problems: one in the downtown region, and the other in midtown. The subway route, which ran from south to north, would encounter plenty of schist.

Although other geological formations (such as quicksand, soft rock, and rubble) would prove irksome to subway engineers, it was the schist that engineers worried about. Not only is the rock extremely difficult to cut through, it is not uniformly hard. Schist is susceptible to decay. It can fracture or collapse, often without warning. Schist is unpredictable and thus dangerous to work with.

Then there was the reality that Manhattan Island is not flat. Although most of the island below 96th Street is reasonably level, the Upper West Side can rise as high as 200 feet above sea level. It also includes wide valleys, some of which would require span-ning with viaducts.

The basic decision confronting Parsons from the outset was whether to go deep or to remain close to the surface. Deep tun-neling had its advantages. If the rock was solid, little in the way of a support structure would be required to dig it out and keep it in place. Furthermore, if the tunneling were dug deep enough, it would be well below the man-made infrastructure (for example, building foundations, water, sewer, gas, and electrical lines) that existed in all but a few parts of the city.

Digging deep meant that stations would require elevators to take passengers from the surface to the tracks below. Elevators large enough to carry so many people would be difficult to install, expensive to maintain, and time consuming to use. Besides, no one was quite sure how many New Yorkers would be

BUILDING AMERICA NOW

BAY AREA RAPID TRANSIT (BART)

In 1962, San Francisco–area voters approved a plan for Bay Area Rapid Transit. Construction of what would eventually total 104 miles (167.3 km) of surface, elevated, and subway track began in 1964. BART carried its first passengers in 1972.

The BART system includes the Transbay Tube, a 3.6-mile (5.7 km), twin-section, concrete and steel, underwater tunnel tube that crosses the San Francisco Bay. The system's trains are powered through a third rail by 1,000 volts of direct current. BART consists of 450 cars (which cost $163 million) built by Rohr, the French firm SOFERVAL, and the Morrison-Knudson Corporation. BART trains can reach speeds of 80 miles (128.7 km) per hour, though they average 33 miles (53.1 km) per hour, including 20-second station stops.

The cost of the basic BART system was $1.4 billion. The cost of the Transbay Tube totaled $176 million. Federal grants provided approximately $330 million of the funds.

BART trains operate between 4:00 A.M. and midnight, Monday through Friday; between 6:00 A.M. and midnight on Saturday; and between 8:00 A.M. and midnight on Sunday. On weekdays, the trains run approximately every 15 minutes.

willing to enter a hole in the ground—let alone 100 or more feet below the surface.

Alhough it would cost a great deal (because of the need to divert a massive infrastructure already in place), Parsons and his engineers decided early on that they would dig the New York Subway route with shallow excavation—the "cut and cover" method—wherever possible. Doing so meant staying close to the surface, in most cases digging no farther than 15 feet (4.5 m) down. Essentially they planned, wherever possible, to tear up the streets, dig a huge trench 15 feet deep by 55 feet (16.7 m) wide, and build a post-and-lintel, steel-column-and-girder framework along its length. The street would then be put back in place over a concrete-covered ceiling.

On paper it all sounded fairly simple and straightforward, just as John McDonald had said. In reality, however, constructing the New York Subway under Contracts One and Two would turn out to be one of the most complex and difficult civil engineering challenges of all time.

CHAPTER 3

Beneath
the Surface

Construction of the New York Subway took place concurrently at various locations along the planned 22-mile (35.4 km) route. Where rock was relatively malleable—where it could be picked away fairly easily or blasted apart with little effort—the "cut and cover" construction method was preferred. Streets were torn up and rectangular trenches gouged out. Massive timbering in the ditches, with cross bracings, rangers, and posts, was often needed to support on-surface decking used to cover sidewalks and thoroughfares. This was necessary so that the daily business of the city, getting about on foot and in surface trolleys, could continue relatively unimpeded.

Workers, mostly unskilled laborers, would begin by clawing at street pavement with pickaxes. As the rubble of broken brick, stone, rock, and asphalt piled up, it was shoveled into wheelbarrows and hauled away. In some cases, pushcarts that ran as temporary, small-gauged railroads moved material out.

Actual subway construction could now commence. First, a four-inch concrete foundation was poured over the floor and then covered with hot asphalt to keep water from seeping up. Walls were constructed of *terra cotta* (baked clay), with holes running throughout their length. Electrical conduit would be strung through these openings at a later date. Concrete footings were next placed on the surface bed, five feet (1.5 m) apart. These would support the tunnel skeleton, which consisted of I-beam posts and girders. Finally, concrete inner walls and a ceiling were poured. The basic subway was complete—John McDonald's elongated "cellar" in the making.

That was the so-called easy part, except for one thing. Engineers had decided early on to avoid, if at all possible, tunneling under buildings, lest foundations give way and structures collapse. Instead, they would follow the line of existing streets, where they reasoned there would be better ventilation for construction crews and less danger of permanent property damage.

Yet, Manhattan at the turn of the twentieth century (even in its northern regions) was relatively built up, with a mass of underground utilities to contend with. As Vivian Heller observed in *The City Beneath Us: Building the New York Subways*:

> Because the subway was often built close to the surface of the street, its construction involved the relocation of underground pipes and ducts. Sewers, water and gas mains, steam pipes, pneumatic tubes, and electric conduits were tightly packed together just beneath the trolley tracks, which took up the streets. The first phase of subway construction entailed rerouting and rebuilding this maze of existing pipes and structures, often without the benefit of utility line maps.

It certainly did not help that sewer pipes, which extended up to three feet (.9 m) in diameter, ran east and west across Manhattan so that waste could be discharged into the Hudson and East rivers. The subway route moved north and south, at a right angle to these interfering drainage carriers.

As troublesome, difficult, and frustrating as it was to remove and replace city utilities, engineers still found cut and cover the

So-called sandhogs used their bare hands, pickaxes, and dynamite to excavate tunnels for the subway under the rivers of New York City. These underground workers were at risk for the bends, a medical condition related to fluctuations in atmospheric pressure. *Above*, sandhogs dig a subway tunnel running underneath the East River.

preferred way to proceed wherever possible. Unfortunately, only slightly more than half (52 percent) of the subway's total length could be cut using this surface excavation method. The reason was clear, as Clifton Hood explained in *722 Miles*:

Due to the island's hilly topography, abrupt changes in the ground level occurred so frequently that the use of cut and cover would not have kept the rails at grade. To prevent the IRT from resembling a Coney Island roller coaster, the RTC had to build a wide variety of structures, including a 2,174-foot steel arch viaduct across Manhattan Valley between 122nd and 135th streets and rock tunnels in Murray Hill and upper Manhattan.

Construction was about to get much tougher.

MINING THE SUBWAY

Tunnel boring—where workers first dig vertical shafts and then proceed horizontally, either on land or under a river—would constitute approximately 13 percent of the subway's 22-mile (35.4 km) route under Contract One, which was signed in 1900. (Contract Two, signed in 1902, would take subway construction south from City Hall to South Ferry, and then under the East River to Brooklyn.)

Such tunneling, whether on Manhattan Island itself or under rivers, was essentially a mining operation. Miners, who were mostly experienced members of workers' unions, were required to do the digging and blasting. For the tunnel under Washington Heights, from 168th Street to 181st Street, a two-mile-long (3.2 km) cavity had to be bored, often at a depth of 150 feet (45.7 m). On completion, elevators would be required to take passengers to and from a station platform above.

Construction on this structure, which came to be known as the Fort George Tunnel, attracted more than 600 miners, many from out west and as far away as South Africa. Many of these miners, who were accustomed to working in rural and isolated areas, found digging in Manhattan an unusual undertaking with unfamiliar advantages and pleasures. According to the *New York Times*, in an interview conducted in 1901, one miner declared,

> In the old country, a miner was a countryman, isolated far from even small towns in most cases, and rarely, if ever, able to enjoy urban pleasures. But here—ah! One could mine by day and carouse by night, the distance from the bowels of the earth to the theater was nothing, the possibility of diversion was limited only by the amount of one's daily wages and one's capacity for doing without sleep.

Mining operations went well enough as long as the schist encountered was stable. Carving consisted of an endlessly repeating cycle of drilling, blasting, clearing, and timbering of a relatively small-diameter bore until two headings came together at the middle, thus completing the basic tunnel. Workers then enlarged the tube to full bore, lined it with concrete, and set the track and support utilities.

When rock softened or became permeated with water—either on the island itself (because Manhattan is essentially at sea level) or under rivers—the situation could become unstable and dangerous. To keep the water at bay, a tunnel had to be pressurized. Air was pumped in until the pressure was high enough to counter the water pressure and keep the liquid back. Miners who labored in such conditions (known as "working in air") would often experience pressures two or three times what their bodies were used to. These risk takers, referred to as "sandhogs," had to stop for frequent rests. Often they labored no more that half an hour before "retiring" to an air chamber brought up to atmospheric pressure to recuperate.

Clearly, subway work was not for the faint of heart. Danger struck most cruelly at the portal to the Fort George Tunnel on October 24, 1903. According to Lorraine Diehl, writing in *Subways*:

It was close to ten P.M. when a gang of twenty-two sandhogs, who had spent the day blasting through the solid schist, planted their dynamite sticks and followed foreman Timothy Sullivan to the surface. With only a few hundred feet to go, everyone was anxious to get the job done. It had been standard procedure to set off two dynamite blasts for rock tunneling, but on this stretch of tunnel, the contractor ordered three blasts. He had apparently not taken into account the fragility of the rock, made porous by underground springs. . . . After hearing the three explosions, the workers followed Sullivan back into the tunnel area. Suddenly there were three more blasts, probably from unexploded dynamite. The weakened tunnel roof gave

HARLEM RENAISSANCE:
Ready to Stomp

The New York Subway, in particular the original Interborough Rapid Transit, literally created Harlem. When fine apartments sprang up in northern Manhattan in anticipation of a huge middle-class white influx that never materialized, black families moved in and filled the void. Coupled with the Great Migration from the racially segregated and repressive South, which saw 750,000 African Americans migrate north in the third decade of the twentieth century, Harlem began to fill up—fast. By the mid-1920s, Harlem—with 175,000 people and covering just three miles (4.8 km)—had become home to the largest concentration of blacks in the world.

At the time, creative expression was one of the few avenues open to African Americans in a vibrant Roaring Twenties city. The result was an artistic, cultural, and intellectual awakening known first as the New Negro Movement and, later, the Harlem Renaissance. Critic Alain Locke called it "a spiritual coming of age, in which the black community was able to seize upon its first chances for group expression and self determination."

Musically, the Harlem Renaissance brought together, as Nikki Giovanni declared, "a gaggle of Blacks who sang their plantation songs and then made a variation called *blues* and then made a variation called *jazz*." Black-owned magazines and newspapers flourished, "freeing African Americans from the constricting influences of mainstream white society," Beth Rowen explained. In these magazines, Langston Hughes, Countee Cullen, and W.E.B. DuBois found full expression for their wide-ranging thoughts. In the visual arts, artists such as Aaron Douglas sought to overcome negative images perpetrated in movies such as *Birth of a Nation* and, later, *Gone with the Wind*. Through the Harlem Renaissance, blacks fought not only to heighten a cultural awareness for themselves but to influence whites in seeking greater acceptance.

way, loosening a three-hundred-ton boulder that came bounding down on the workers below. Ten men lost their lives, including the foreman.

Forty-four more workers would die before the first phase of subway construction was completed in October 1904.

SANDHOGS UNDERWATER

Rock tunneling, or digging deep on the island of Manhattan, was one task; boring beneath rivers was quite another. Contract One required builders to go below the 750-foot-wide (228.6 m) Harlem River to cross into the Bronx. Under Contract Two, they would have to span the much wider, nearly 2,000-foot (609.6 m) East River on their way to Brooklyn. Dramatically different methods were used to affect the crossings.

To build the two-track Lenox Avenue line under the Harlem River, the contractor chose to fabricate giant cast-iron tubes made from individual plates, assemble sections, and then float them into the Harlem River. Once the tubes were positioned over a pre-dredged site, they were filled with water, sunk into place, and secured. This method had many advantages, including that it permitted much closer spacing between tunnels.

For the first subway into Brooklyn (completed in 1908 as part of the Contract Two extension), boring deep and using a shield was the method of choice. The shield, which was made of 2.125-inch-thick (5.39 cm) steel plates and weighed almost 200 tons (181.4 metric tonnes), was designed to provide a cutting edge and, at the same time, protect frontline workers from falling rock. It also had to resist the crushing forces of the earth and rock around it, while slowly inching forward under tremendous pressure. David Weitzman, author of *A Subway for New York*, provided the details:

> The front of the shield formed a sharp cutting edge and a hood to protect the drillers from falling rocks. At the back were compressed-air-powered rams, which exerted over six million

pounds of force. After the sandhogs had cleared a space in front of the shield, the rams extended and pushed the entire shield forward. Each time the shield moved forward, a space was left behind just wide enough for another ring of cast iron. These rings became the permanent tunnel.

Digging in such an environment below a riverbed was dangerous work, and accidents did happen. Fortunately, not all resulted in serious injuries or fatalities. Indeed, one in particular took a most bizarre turn.

Construction on the two-track line that ran under the Harlem River veered away from the usual method of excavation. Instead of having workers clear away dirt, the contractor used steel plates to create a giant tube that was placed in the bottom of the Harlem River when completed. *Above*, workers sink steel tubes in the Harlem River for the subway tunnel.

Marshall Mabey was working in a compressed-air tunnel when, all of a sudden, it deflated like a punctured balloon. Mabey was sucked up through several feet of thick sand and blasted out above the river on a geyser of water 40 feet (12.19 m) high. "I closed my eyes and managed to get my hands over my head when I realized I was in sand and was being pushed by a tremendous force," the astonished worker declared a short time later, as reported by Vivian Heller. "I was being squeezed tighter than any girl ever held me and the pressure was all over me, especially on my head. . . . The last thing I recalled was seeing the Brooklyn Bridge above me while I was whirling around in the air."

Mabey went back to work later that afternoon.

During subway digging, it was not surprising for workers to uncover strange objects from the past. At Dyckman Street, bones of a prehistoric mastodon were unearthed. Elsewhere, the hull of an old Dutch ship that had gone down in 1613 was exhumed, as were old parts of the city, such as Cat Alley. Digging down brought much of New York's past back up for reexamination.

TEARING IT UP

Although every attempt was made to avoid tunneling under buildings, monuments, or other structures, there were times when it was unavoidable. A subway tunnel that passed directly under the Hotel Belmont at 42nd Street and Park Avenue, for example, had to be shored up with extra-heavy girders and foundations to support both the hotel and the subway station.

A particularly difficult challenge arose when it was discovered that the subway would pass under the east side of the Columbus Monument, in what is now Columbus Circle, at the southwest corner of Central Park. The monument—which stood 75 feet (22.86 m) tall and weighed 700 tons (635 metric tonnes)—was built in 1892 to commemorate the four-hundredth anniversary of Columbus's landfall in the New World. The subway was designed to pass within three feet (.9 m) of the monument's center, which would reduce a significant portion of its support. According to the Web site ConstructionCompany.com:

> In order to ensure the safety of the monument and the workers, a tunnel six feet wide and seven feet high was dug under the monument just outside the subway's wall line. Workers put in a concrete bottom in order to support a row of wooden posts that would carry the footing above. When this was done, the tunnel was filled with masonry rubble, making a wall that was strong enough to support the monument during the subway's construction.

A unique situation also developed in Times Square (so named when the *New York Times* moved its headquarters there) at 42nd Street and Broadway in 1904. The pressroom of the newspaper was actually located below the subway. The subway had to be built right through the building, with the building's columns passing through a subway station. Workers used steel channels to brace the building and ensure it was not damaged.

The shoring up of nearby buildings and elevated train tracks was required in numerous places to prevent structures tumbling down from subway digging. However, before construction actually commenced, the IRT hired photographers to go up and down the projected subway route and photograph every single structure. This provided a visual record of exactly what was there and what it looked like before digging, blasting, and timbering took place. If any property owner later claimed damages from the IRT, a photograph could be used to set the record straight.

As well planned and carefully executed as the massive subway construction project was, there were failures; in some places, everything came tumbling down. Wooden streets occasionally collapsed, with streetcars, wagons, and even pedestrians falling in. A cut-and-cover ditch would simply cave in and delay construction in the given location for weeks.

A particularly frustrating cave-in occurred on the east side of Park Avenue between 37th and 38th streets. The disaster caused so much damage to nearby property that August Belmont felt it would be better to buy out all the owners as a group rather than attempt to compensate them individually. He pur-

BUILDING AMERICA NOW

METROPOLITAN ATLANTA RAPID TRANSIT AUTHORITY (MARTA)

Atlanta came late to mass transit; the city did not create a regional authority until 1965. With the establishment of the Metropolitan Atlanta Rapid Transit Authority, the region got moving—literally. In February 1972, MARTA purchased the Atlanta Transit System for $12.9 million and took control of the area's primary bus transportation system. Throughout the 1970s, MARTA received $800 million from the federal government for planning, design, land acquisition, and construction of a rapid rail system. The first MARTA trains began to run on June 30, 1979.

Actual MARTA subway construction commenced in 1980, and the first line opened two years later, in September 1982. MARTA now had 9 miles (14.48 km) of track. Expansion of the system continued in the 1990s, when a heavy construction program was begun in anticipation of the 1996 Olympic Games.

As with Boston's subway system, MARTA in the 1990s focused on its transit's link to community development through a Transit Oriented Development, or TOD, program. The idea was to create a live, work, and play community built around a rail station. By 2000, MARTA's TOD program was considered to be the largest multiuse development of its kind in the United States.

chased the entire block for $1 million and then demolished all the buildings.

Difficulties aside, in late 1904—as the end of the four-and-a-half-year construction period neared—August Belmont and company had much to celebrate. Fifty-eight miles (93.3 km) of track (open trench, underground, and elevated) were laid, and a good portion of the route was four tracks wide. There would be 43 local stations and 5 express stations. Some trains were expected to achieve speeds of up to 45 miles (72.4 km) per hour, more than three times as fast as any elevated could go. Power to run the subway trains and light the stations would be supplied by a massive IRT powerhouse built on the Hudson River. The station would generate more electricity from its 10 steam engines, driving giant dynamos, than any power plant yet built.

GOING SUBWAY MAD

Initially, given New York's response on opening day, October 27, 1904, and in the days and weeks to come, enthusiasm for the subway knew no bounds. From the mayor on down, New Yorkers simply went "subway mad."

With early afternoon dignitary speechmaking (suffered through by a crowd of 10,000 that stretched from City Hall to the Brooklyn Bridge) mercifully completed around 2:30 P.M., New York's mayor, George B. McClellan, descended into City Hall's signature subway station and promptly took control, literally, of a waiting subway train.

In a ceremonial gesture, McClellan was supposed to drive the first subway train for a brief moment—carefully edging it forward—and then turn control over to the official motorman. The mayor, however, refused to surrender "his" train. He was having too much fun. "I'm running this train!" the mayor shouted to the trainload of dignitaries on board. He took off, often careening around curves at speeds of 40 miles (64.3 km) per hour. Officials were in a panic; if the train derailed on opening day, that image would keep New Yorkers out of the subway for a

The building of the New York City Subway was not without accidents. Occasionally, wooden crossbeams and steel girders collapsed, causing unlucky pedestrians, wagons, and streetcars to fall into construction sites. These cave-ins were dangerous, time consuming, and costly, as they caused damage to the surrounding area and delayed work for weeks. *Above*, a cave-in at Seventh Avenue.

long time. Finally, at 103rd Street, the mayor handed control over to IRT authorities. "Afterward," as reported by Clifton Hood, "the 'Motorman Mayor,' as he was now called, attributed his success to his mastery of 'automobiling.' "

When the subway finally opened its doors to the general public at 7:00 P.M., the crush and excitement was uncontrollable. "Crowds stormed the entrances, parting with their five-cent fares as they pressed down onto the platforms to await the train," Lorraine Diehl reported. "Some had come from Brooklyn, others from New Jersey, to take the first ride. From seven until sometime after midnight, over 120,000 people rode the subway on that Thursday evening, descending onto the platforms at a rate of 25,000 an hour."

New York had become "the city of human prairie dogs," the *Utica Saturday Globe* reported. "Just like the little burrowers of the west darting into their holes." On Sunday, the only day many New Yorkers had off, close to a million people tried to board the new system, which was designed to carry a maximum of 350,000. Lines wound around blocks; waiting times to board often stretched to over two hours. "Doing the subway" became the "in" thing. Many rode the underground trains for hours, dressed in their Sunday best—a new form of recreation in the making.

Before the year was out, the Subway Express Two-Step, a dance that mimicked the motion of a subway car, had taken hold. The song "Down in the Subway," by Jean Schwartz and William Jerome, described New Yorkers' new place to flirt:

Down in the Subway,
Oh, what a place!
Under the isle of Manhattan, speeding through space
Just the place for spooning,
All the season 'round,
Way down, way down in the Subway
Underneath the ground.

Early complaints of dizziness, fainting spells, and nausea aside, New Yorkers had taken to their new form of rapid transit with great enthusiasm. During the first year alone, 106 million people rode the subway. Clearly, Belmont and company had a great deal to smile about. So, it would seem, did New Yorkers.

CHAPTER 4

Outward Bound

When Mayor George McClellan brought his opening day joy-ride to an end at the IRT's 103rd Street station, and a motorman took over to pilot the five-car train on to 145th Street, that was the end of the subway line—but only for the inaugural run. During the next few years, still more subway mileage would open up. On November 26, 1904, track was extended to Bronx Park. Service expanded to South Ferry on July 10, 1905. Train lines pushed on to Brooklyn (through the East River tunnel) in January 1908, and the subway reached 242nd Street and Broadway on August 1 of that same year. The Interborough Rapid Transit subway project, eight years in the making, was at last complete.

For New Yorkers, there was much to be proud of. Despite their colorful tile mosaics, natural vault lighting, and oak ticket booths, most of the 43 subway stations were rather spartan; the flagship City Hall station, however, was a work apart, a true civic monument. Designed by the architectural firm of Heins & LaFarge, the station was, as described by Clifton Hood, "an underground chapel in the round that had beautiful Guastavino arches, leaded glass skylights, and chandeliers." The station left travelers spellbound.

Of the remaining 42 subway stations, the majority were decorated with ceramic bas-relief name panels that depicted neighborhood themes, all the better to be easily recognized by non-English-speaking immigrants. Columbus Circle, for example, displayed Christopher Columbus's flagship, the *Santa Maria*.

The kiosks, which covered subway entrances and exits, were of equal delight. Clearly designed to seduce riders into a subterranean world (one still alien to most New Yorkers), the kiosk "was a fanciful structure of cast-iron and glass with an elegantly rounded roof borrowed from the *kushks*, or 'summerhouses,' of ancient Turkey and Persia," as Lorraine Diehl declared in her book *Subways*. The intricately fabricated kiosks soon became an IRT trademark.

Of course, beautiful entrances and attractive stations all led to one place—the subway train. The first subway cars were "composites," so called because, although they had steel frames, their sides were made of wood. "Good looking cars inside and out, their white ash exteriors were finished in a deep, rich, wine color," declared Brian Cudahy. "The sides of the cars were slightly tapered, making them narrower at the top than at the bottom. They measured 51 feet, 2 inches [15.5 m] in overall length, 8 feet, 11–7/8 inches [2.5 m] wide at the windowsills, and just a fraction of an inch over 12 feet [3.65 m] high. Each car was equipped with 52 seats made of attractive rattan."

Indeed, August Belmont had his own uniquely crafted "fantasy car" that he could ride in at any time. Parked on a siding at his Belmont Hotel and entered through a private passageway, the Mineola, as it was named, cost more than $11,000 to build. According to Lorraine Diehl:

> Its luxurious interior reflected the exorbitant price tag: walls were of natural mahogany with brass trim and the arched Empire ceiling was bathed in a tinted pistachio green. Velvet

drapes and cut-glass wall vases filled with fresh flowers framed stained-glass windows. The Mineola had its own lavatory, a linen closet, a steward's galley, a kitchen, and a bar where champagne was kept chilled. Built-in leather chairs provided the utmost comfort.

BUILDING AMERICA NOW

LOS ANGELES METRO

Los Angeles—never known for mass transit, given its car-culture persona—nonetheless has one of the largest population centers that must be serviced by some form of pubic transit. More than nine million people—one-third of California's residents—live, work, and play within its 1,433-square-mile (3,711 sq km) service area.

The Los Angeles Metro, in addition to operating more than 2,000 peak-hour buses on an average weekday, has built and operated 73 miles (117.4 km) of rail service, including its Metro Red Line subway system. The Red Line itself, which opened on January 30, 1993, is 17.4 miles (28 km) in length and entirely underground. Total cost of the Red Line subway has been estimated at $5.6 billion.

Red Line trains, powered by a third-rail, 750-volt DC system, race up to 70 miles (112.6 km) per hour underneath the Santa Monica Mountains. Each of the Red Line's 108 vehicles costs $1.5 million, extends 75 feet (22.8 m) in length, and weighs 82,000 pounds (37,194 kg).

The Red Line, from its conception, has incorporated extensive art into its stations. One half of one percent of rail construction costs were allocated to the creation of original artworks. Described as one of the most imaginative public arts programs in the country, the Los Angeles Metro has received numerous design and artistic excellence awards. More than 250 artists have been commissioned to do work as part of the Metro's arts program.

Evidently, one of Belmont's greatest pleasures was to take friends on private subway rides throughout "his" system, the New York Subway that he had financed and seen to completion.

SOMETHING TO SHOUT ABOUT

Although many New Yorkers obviously admired, praised, and even loved their new underground mode of rapid transit, it did not take them long to start complaining about everything from bad air to bad art.

"Women Faint in Bad Subway Atmosphere" read a *New York Times* headline of November 6, 1904, less than 10 days after the IRT began operation. "Foul air and nervousness due to the excitement of the trip, it being her first over the road," a doctor and fellow passenger commented about one woman's "ordeal." A number of riders complained of headaches, attacks of vertigo, dizziness, and occasional fainting spells, all of which evidently resulted from either a lack of oxygen or the poor quality of what oxygen there was.

The IRT's official response was that, given enough time, all would be righted. "Lack of Oxygen?" the company line went, as quoted in the *Times*, "That is beyond us; a matter for the scientists to play with. . . . This will all pass away when the newness of the road has worn away and the subway gets fairly aired out."

But bad air wasn't the only problem. On the second day of subway service, holes were being pounded into station walls so that advertising posters could be put up. "Public opinion should be encouraged to express itself freely on the subject of the unsightly and dangerous advertising which is to disfigure the subway stations," the *New York Times* opined in November 1904. "It is a nuisance, and public opinion demands its suppression."

Perhaps! But under Contract One, the right to display such "vulgar commercialism," as Michael Brooks put it, was perfectly legal. "The worthy and eminently respectable gentlemen who are making all this outcry are simply out of touch with the times,"

On October 27, 1904, a ceremony commemorating the completion of the New York City Subway was held outside City Hall. New York City mayor George McClellan then invited important financiers and dignitaries to join him on the inaugural subway ride *(above)*. Afterwards, boasting the slogan "City Hall to Harlem in 15 minutes!" the subway opened to the public.

an IRT official shot back, as reported in *Under the Sidewalks of New York*. "The masses who struggle for existence, who produce the money upon which their leisurely critics live, get much of their information about what is going on in the business world through reading the signs arranged for their entertainment upon the walls of the subway." The subway ads stayed—and have never left.

Bad air and bad art aside, it was IRT overcrowding that most irritated commuters. The *New York Times* identified train car doors as the main culprit. "The doors are too narrow and the congestion which occurs at every station when the streams of incoming and outgoing passengers strive to pass each other in what would be scant room for the movement one way, makes for confusion, discomfort, and delay."

In the months to come, such overcrowding would only get worse. By late November 1904, the IRT already carried 125,000 more passengers per day than it had been designed to ferry.

Discomfort, although not to be discounted, was one thing. A dangerous subway, however, was quite another.

In one respect, subway danger wasn't the IRT's fault. They could hardly be blamed for failing to prevent people from attempting to outrun a fast-moving train. Train runners and dodgers, accustomed to the poky trolleys and els—the latter of which traveled at barely 13 miles (20.9 km) per hour—were no match for subway trains that sped up to 40 miles (64.3 km) per hour. That said, one fatality in particular did not have to happen. In August 1910, S. Silvio, answering the call of nature, ducked into the Times Square tunnel to relieve himself. He never again saw the light of day.

HARLEM IN 15 MINUTES

There was no question about it: Once one made it through the crushing crowds and onto the train, subway travel was fast—lightning fast—especially compared to what had existed before. Indeed, prior to opening day in October 1904, IRT officials claimed that their subway would rush New Yorkers from City Hall to Harlem, an eight-mile (12.8 km) journey uptown, in just 15 minutes. As the subway gained acceptance as the new rapid transit, Harlem quickly became the "in" destination, though not for the upper-middle-class white residents it was originally intended to attract.

Housing speculators, on hearing of the subway's planned route into Harlem, quickly built (overbuilt, actually) some of the finest apartment houses in the city there. According to Laban Carrick Hill in *Harlem Stomp: A Cultural History of the Harlem*

Renaissance, "By 1902, whole buildings remained unoccupied as they waited for the expected flood of tenants, which would not come for another two years. Facing financial ruin, developers went begging for tenants. At dire times like these, economic necessity can override racial prejudice."

Soon enough, a smart, entrepreneurial 24-year-old African American named Philip A. Payton Jr. was on the scene, offering landlords a rental rate above the depressed real estate price. Payton knew that middle-class blacks, then living in squalid conditions in Midtown's "Black Bohemia," would pay almost anything to move uptown.

The rest, as they say, is history. "Neither Payton nor the white property owners could have seen what was to come—the wholesale migration of blacks from downtown Manhattan to Harlem," observed Hill. "Nor could Payton have imagined the extent of the outrage of whites over a few black families' moving into that segregated community."

Payton, of course, was not the only speculator to see gold in the region above New York's 96th Street. Charles T. Barney, exploiting his inside knowledge of the IRT's future route when he became the company's director in 1900, organized a syndicate and quickly spent nearly $7 million to buy up property in Harlem, Washington Heights, Fort George, Inwood, and the Bronx. To speedily recoup its investment, the syndicate took to building what were referred to as "new-law tenements." According to the *New York World*, such housing formed "a distinctive subway zone of flat houses that made the Bronx synonymous with low-income housing."

That said, the new Bronx housing was a step up from what Lower East Side residents had endured for decades. According to Clifton Hood, "By contrast, the new-law tenements going up in the Bronx seemed wonderful. For $16.00 to $20.00 dollars a month residents could rent a brand-new apartment that included two bedrooms, a combined dining-living room, a kitchen with hot water and a gas range, and an interior toilet and bathtub. These new-law tenements had good heating and lighting, carpeted hall-ways, and tastefully decorated foyers and facades."

The subway began to facilitate just the type of upward and outward mobility many New Yorkers were desperate to achieve.

24/7:
Always Rolling

Comparing subway systems worldwide is not easy; knowing what criteria to use is the main challenge. For example, although the New York Subway carries an impressive 1.4 billion passengers a year, that figure places it in third place, behind Tokyo at 2.7 billion and Moscow at 3.2 billion. Yet, when the number of stations is counted, New York leads with 483, followed by Tokyo with 276 and London with 275. When tallying cars, furthermore, one city stands far above the others: New York has a whopping 6,400, London 3,954, and Tokyo 3,609.

In another statistic, New York stands supreme: The New York Subway provides a ride anytime one wants it. London runs its trains from 5:00 A.M. to 1:00 A.M., Tokyo from 5:00 A.M. to 12:15 A.M., and Moscow from 6:00 A.M. to 1:00 A.M. No other system can match New York's—its trains run 24 hours a day, 7 days a week, 52 weeks a year. In New York, one can always catch a ride, day or night.

Of course, the number of New York Subway riders varies dramatically throughout a 24-hour period. Between 2:00 A.M. and 3:00 A.M. on a typical weekday, the system averages only 6 persons per car. Between 7:00 A.M. and 8:00 A.M., that number leaps to 85 persons, often jammed into what is known as the "crush load." During the evening rush hour (beginning at 4:00 P.M.), the number rises again, to 68 per car, but not to the morning rush hour number of 85 persons. It seems that many New Yorkers, having completed a hard day's work, choose to stay in town and enjoy the city's pleasures, taking the subway home at a later time.

Lower and middle Manhattan were not neglected as a result of the subway's northern advance, however. Indeed, Times Square, with its own subway stop and the arrival of the new *New York Times* headquarters, was fast becoming the city's first twentieth-century social and cultural center. Before 1904, legitimate theaters in Manhattan had been clustered around Herald Square at 34th Street and Broadway. The city's els had served Herald Square fairly well, bringing patrons to the theater district to attend a variety of live shows. Yet, with the opening of the subway in 1904, which could more easily transport theatergoers to their night-out destinations, theaters began to relocate to 42nd Street and Broadway. Famed songwriter George M. Cohan was quick to note the change in his well-known song lyrics:

Give my regards to Broadway,
Remember me to Herald Square.
Tell all the gang at 42nd Street
That I will soon be there.

SUBWAY EXPANSION

That the New York Subway was proving to be immensely popular left little doubt. By 1908, the underground averaged 800,000 nickel-paying passengers a day—a third more than planned. As with any public transit system, the rush hour was the part that caused overflow and crowding. One-third of all travelers were on the subway between the two-hour peak periods from 8:00 A.M. to 10:00 A.M. and 4:00 P.M. to 6:00 P.M. For many, the commute had become decidedly unpleasant. Spitting, it seems, was a particularly annoying habit commuters faced. One rider, Erwin de Kohler, complained to the *New York Times*:

I have become accustomed to the crowding and the pushing and all the discomforts that are the natural consequence of the herding of hundreds of people in a confined space, but there is one thing I cannot tolerate . . . that is . . . "spitting."

The answer to such subway crunching would appear to be to build more tracks—to add parallel lines in Manhattan and additional ones into the boroughs. Belmont, however, was opposed.

To the financier, and the now undisputed "Subway King," the crowding of his railcars was a good thing; more riders meant more money. "If the day ever comes when transportation during rush hours is done without crowding, the companies doing it will fail financially," he is to have said, as quoted by Clifton Hood. To Belmont, "The profits were in the straps"; *straps* were those "extra" riders (straphangers) who were forced to stand and hang on to the overhead straps.

The riding public—which meant most New Yorkers—was getting impatient and frustrated, and it soon began to agitate for serious subway expansion. Belmont, however, held back. With his capture of the city's streetcar lines and all four elevateds, through a clever merger that formed the Interborough-Metropolitan, Belmont literally owned all of Manhattan's mass transit. In response to his rock-solid transit monopoly, the newly formed Public Service Commission (PSC) drew up plans for a brand-new subway, to be known as the Triborough. Belmont, it seemed, would finally have some competition.

The Triborough was to have three major routes: one each in Manhattan, the Bronx, and Brooklyn. Progressives of the era hoped the Triborough would decentralize the city's population and break the Interborough subway monopoly. Yet, would investors be willing to put up the huge sums of money necessary to construct and operate subway lines into what, in effect, was considered the outer borough "sticks," where there was no assurance that riders could be found in sufficient numbers to recover costs and make a profit?

On October 20, 1910, when the PSC opened the first set of bids to construct the new subway, they got their answer. Not a single company submitted a proposal. Twenty-three companies offered to build the new Triborough system in a second round of bids—but with municipal funds. The city would not go for that.

A ladies-only car *(above)* was introduced to the subway system to acclimate female riders to underground transport and spare them contact with unsavory characters. Accompanied by an attendant *(center, rear)*, women could enjoy a comfortable subway ride without having to compete with men for seats or hanging straps.

Belmont, however, had by now received the message. If he did not agree to expand his Interborough subway, some entity would eventually build a new, competing system. On December 5, 1910, the IRT finally came up with an expansion proposal. It would form an "H" route that would give expanded and dramatically improved service to the Bronx. According to Clifton Hood, the plans "included two new subways that would connect with the original Contract No. 1 line. One would go down the west side from the IRT's Time Square stop to the Battery and across the East River to Brooklyn. The other route would go up Lexington Avenue from Grand Central Terminal to the Bronx."

However, before authorities met to review the IRT proposal, the Brooklyn Rapid Transit (BRT) company stepped up to the plate. In search of a piece of the Manhattan subway pie, the BRT had a plan of its own to present.

THE DUAL CONTRACTS

The BRT was, by 1911, a major moneymaking transit corporation that controlled nearly all of the elevated and street railway lines in Brooklyn. As effective as the BRT was in its home borough, however, it could not get its passengers into Manhattan. BRT lines ended at ferry terminals on the Brooklyn side of the East River. The company desperately wanted a route (or routes) over or under that river.

It was not just a toehold that the Brooklyn intruder sought. The BRT yearned to penetrate deep into the island, even if it meant paralleling IRT lines. By 1911, it was clear that Manhattan was developing a prosperous business center in midtown. The BRT craved a piece of the transit pie that would deliver commuters in and out of the new, up-and-coming commercial area.

Furthermore, the BRT had been angered when the IRT, under Contract Two, extended a line into Brooklyn—as far as Flatbush and Atlantic avenues—in 1908. If the IRT could have a chunk of Brooklyn, why was the BRT not allowed a piece of Manhattan? Besides, the BRT was eager to stretch its transit expertise into subway operations. The BRT, officials claimed, could build and operate a subway, too—maybe even better than the IRT.

In the end, the city of New York declined to accept either the IRT or the BRT proposal. Instead, after months and months of negotiation that produced a document six inches thick, an agreement was reached that would give both companies entrée into each other's territories while greatly expanding subway mileage as a whole. The new arrangement, known as the Dual Contracts (because they were signed by two separate, private companies, the IRT and the BRT, and the city), was made official on March 19, 1913. It promised to take New York City rapid transit to a whole new level.

The agreement called for the city of New York to put up $164 million, with the IRT contributing $77 million and the BRT $61 million. For a total of what would eventually be $352 million, New York would see its rapid-transit network more than double, from 296 to 619 miles. There would be complications, of course. To accommodate large el trains on its new subway lines, the BRT trains (and tunnels) would be bigger than those of the IRT. As a result, BRT trains could not clear smaller IRT tunnels. As Clifton Hood pointed out, "If the two subway systems were ever unified, this mismatch would prevent integration with the old lines and prohibit joint orders for rolling stock."

By late 1918, with the Great War in Europe concluding, the Dual Contract companies had finally completed their upgrades and extensions. Rapid transit had spread to all of the boroughs but Staten Island. Although both the IRT and the BRT were, by this time, under severe financial strain as a result of what some claimed was overreaching (as well as mismanagement), New York had achieved a true city-wide mass-transit system. Then, on November 1, 1918, tragedy struck, the result of which would alter transit in the city for decades to come.

CHAPTER 5

Subway Carnage

By 1918, five years after the Dual Contracts were signed, New Yorkers had two competing (and, to a considerably lesser extent, cooperating) private subway systems. Combined, the IRT and the BRT provided a total of 619 miles (996 km) of track. The size of the network was incredible. "If a passenger boarded a train at 9:00 one morning and traveled over the entire system at normal speeds, he would not return to his starting point until twenty-one hours later, at 6:00 the following morning," observed Clifton Hood. By the end of World War I, New York City transit lines were carrying an astonishing 2.4 billion riders annually. New York's subway had become the largest rapid-transit system in the world.

That was the good news. There were, however, major problems. By 1918, the IRT and the BRT were in serious financial straits. Both were bleeding money, and both were teetering on the edge of bankruptcy. The nickel fare was the main cause.

When the Dual Contacts were signed, both companies agreed to keep the price of a ride—no matter the distance or the number of transfers—to five cents, and to do it for 49 years into the future, until 1962. The trouble was, by 1919, the nickel of 1904 was worth only 2.6 cents; inflation had eaten into its real value. Yet, IRT and BRT expenses were rising. Between 1916 and 1919, the cost of brake shoes shot up 150 percent. A ton of steel went from $30.00 to $90.00, a ton of coal from $3.23 to $6.07. Wages increased, too. By 1919, the Interborough paid its workers $6 million more than in 1916.

Even with pay raises, employee-employer relations were strained—particularly so within the BRT. The Brooklyn Rapid Transit Company had, for some time, refused to recognize the Brotherhood of Locomotive Engineers as a bargaining union for its motormen. Any motorman suspected of union activity was relentlessly harassed. According to Brian Cudahy in *The Malbone Street Wreck*, "Management officials often followed suspected employees after work; disciplinary action, usually on trumped-up charges, regularly followed any discovery that a worker was active in union affairs—or for that matter, had even dropped by a union hall after supper some evening out of pure curiosity."

With a membership drive by the Brotherhood of Locomotive Engineers in full swing in the summer of 1918, the BRT discharged 40 motormen, approximately 10 percent of the total force. They branded the "troublemakers" as communists. In response, the union called a strike. Motormen and train guards walked off the job at 5:00 A.M. on Friday, November 1, 1918.

Just how effective the union's work stoppage was is open to debate. Brotherhood representatives claimed that 80 percent of the company's motormen and motor switchmen walked out. The BRT disputed that number and spoke of only minor inconveniences. Nonetheless, the company—which had anticipated a strike—rushed into service many employees who had only rudimentary training as motormen. Some had never piloted a passenger-carrying BRT train before, having merely driven trains around yards and terminals as motor switchmen. Such individuals, it would soon become apparent, were ill prepared to handle fully loaded trains—particularly during rush hour and on unfamiliar routes.

Union and BRT representatives, in an attempt to reach a settlement, met at the New York State Public Services Commission's office in Manhattan on Friday evening. At around 7:00 P.M., with both sides making little progress toward agreement, word reached negotiators of a terrible accident on the BRT's Brighton Beach line in Brooklyn, near Prospect Park. A large number of casualties were reported. No one knew at the time that nearly 100 people were dead, and that what happened at 6:42 P.M. on November 1, 1918, would go down as the worst mass-transit disaster in American history.

THE TWO-AND-A-HALF-HOUR MOTORMAN

In the first half of the twentieth century, the man (and it was almost always a man) who operated a train was called a motorman, not an engineer. On the BRT system, such an individual stood in a small compartment (cab) at the front of his train. With his hands on two controls, he accelerated and decelerated the train. There were few automatic features to provide the motorman with backup; running a train was almost entirely a manual operation.

Getting the train to go, by applying current to the motors, was easy enough. Steering was a nonissue, although switching tracks was required at times. Braking, however—the ability to stop a train smoothly in exactly the right spot—took some skill. According to Brian Cudahy, writing in *The Malbone Street Wreck*:

> With train brakes, there is a delay between application and action. . . . It takes many seconds—on a long and fast-moving railroad freight train, it can even be a matter of minutes—for the process to register its full effect. The motorman's ability to anticipate the need for braking action is critical; this ability can only be gained through experience and knowledge—

experience with the way the brakes respond and knowledge of conditions ahead.

To get that experience and training, the BRT would put future motormen through a rather lengthy apprenticeship. First, there was a physical examination. Second, the trainee would sit through a 60-hour course, followed by a 90-question examination. If he passed the exam, he would move on to another 60 hours of apprenticeship aboard regular trains, under the direct supervision of a qualified motorman. More testing and certification would follow, resulting in a minimum of 120 hours of

The job of a subway motorman was not taken lightly. These men were subjected to a lengthy selection and training process. In 1918, when the BRT issued a pay raise for all of its workers but refused to recognize the union that represented most of the motormen working on BRT subways, motormen went on strike. *Above,* a motorman working in the subway.

instruction and training. Even then, the motorman-to-be was only qualified to work around yards and terminals as a motor switchman, with no passengers in the train, until he gained even greater experience.

Twenty-five-year-old Edward Luciano, known to his friends as Billy Lewis, wanted to be a motorman. He had a family and he

MOTORMAN:
Making the Trains Go

A motorman is a person who drives an electrically powered streetcar, locomotive, or subway train. The term has been in use for well over a century, though in the 1970s the designation changed to *engineer* in order to make the job title gender neutral.

As a subway motorman, the train driver's task, above all else, is to transport himself and his passengers safely through the system's miles of track. Critical to doing so is the control the driver has over the train's braking system. Basically, the motorman causes his train to accelerate by the use of a hand-applied throttle control. The driver controls braking with his foot, through the form of a "dead-man" control. The dead-man control is a safety device upon which the driver must exert steady force at all times while driving the train. Should the force applied be interrupted by the motorman's falling asleep, suffering a heart attack, or being held up, the dead-man control is activated. When the driver releases his foot, power to the train is immediately cut and the brakes are applied.

To become a motorman on a New York Subway train, one has to pass a stringent written test in addition to meeting other requirements. In November 2003, approximately 14,000 people showed up to compete for 300 train operator jobs. The test they took included 70 questions and lasted about three and a half hours. Following, according to Kate Ascher, author of *The Works: Anatomy of a City*, are three sample questions used on the test:

had ambition. After all, an experienced motorman could make 50 cents an hour.

In the fall of 1918, Luciano was not a motorman; he was a BRT crew dispatcher. Prior to November 1, he had undergone two and a half hours of classroom instruction as part of a general orientation for the job of motorman. Days before the strike, Luciano

1. Safety rules are most useful because they:
   a. Make it unnecessary to think
   b. Prevent carelessness
   c. Are a guide to avoiding common dangers
   d. Make the worker responsible for any accident

2. The maximum speed permitted when a train is passing through a passenger station without stopping is:
   a. 5 mph
   b. 10 mph
   c. 15 mph
   d. Series speed

3. Third rail power is used to operate the:
   a. Compressors
   b. Emergency car lights
   c. Motorman's indication
   d. Conductor's signal lights

Answers: 1. c, 2. c, 3. a

had spent two days in a train cab with a regular motorman on the BRT's Culver line and Fifth Avenue line; he was anything but a qualified motorman. He should never have been placed in charge of a train full of passengers during rush hour on a line he had not driven before. Yet that is exactly what happened; Luciano, on the night of November 1, 1918, was pressed into service as a strikebreaker to drive a BRT train.

Luciano's "promotion" to motorman is all the more appalling when one considers his health and state of mind the night he was called into service. On Friday, Luciano was still recovering from influenza, a devastating disease that, as a worldwide pandemic, claimed the lives of 50 million people. One of those deaths was Luciano's own three-year-old daughter, who had succumbed only a few days before. To place such a man in control of a five-car train that carried more than 650 people was, clearly, a desperate move on the part of BRT officials. Still, they did it—the result of which was a horrifying tragedy.

FATEFUL RIDE

At 5:15 P.M., on Friday, November 1, 1918, a five-car BRT elevated train pulled out of the Kings Highway yard on the Culver line and headed across the East River to the Park Row terminal on Manhattan Island. Luciano, inexperienced and unqualified as a motorman, was at the controls.

The train comprised five cars, each 50 feet (15.24 m) long. It contained three powered units—cars with electric motors that provided propulsion for the train—and two non-powered trailer cars. The latter lacked motors and were simply hauled along by the other cars. Such a setup was typical of BRT trains in 1918, except for one thing. Correct procedure demanded that the two non-powered trailer cars not be coupled together. Because the trailers weighed 34,000 pounds (15,422 kg) and the powered cars 66,000 pounds (29,937 kg), better balance was achieved when the hookup involved, alternately, a powered car, a trailer, a powered car, a trailer, and a powered car. This, however, was not how

Luciano's train had been coupled. His lead car was a powered unit, followed by two trailers coupled together. The last two cars were powered cars. It was a connection asking for trouble—and it was coming.

Heading inbound from Brooklyn to Manhattan, Luciano guided his train along its route, stopping at the Sands Street station at the Brooklyn end of the Brooklyn Bridge. He then proceeded across the bridge into Manhattan and arrived at the BRT's Manhattan terminal at Park Row, across from City Hall, at 6:08 P.M. At Park Row, the elevated train was figuratively turned around, ready for its outward-bound trip back to Brooklyn and on to Brighton Beach.

Luciano was doing well, showing good train control as he crossed the Brooklyn Bridge heading east. "That he was able to cross the Brooklyn Bridge safely suggests that his lack of experience with the particular configuration of the Brighton Beach Line was his more tragic shortcoming that November evening, not an inability to operate an elevated train on a steep, downhill grade," Brian Cudahy observed in *The Malbone Street Wreck*.

There were delays at various stations, but, at 6:40 P.M., Luciano was ready to leave the Park Place station for Prospect Park. Upon exiting Park Place, an eastbound train encounters a steep downhill grade, a drop of 70 feet (21.3 m). At the bottom of the run was the Malbone Street Tunnel portal, 4,300 feet (1310 m) away. Luciano, unfamiliar with the route he was on, was unaware of the newly installed sharp curve at the entrance to the tunnel he was approaching. A posted sign placed before the curve alerted a motorman to the maximum speed at which he was to take the curve—six miles (9.65 km) per hour. Later, Luciano would tell investigators that, as he entered the curve, his train was traveling at 30 miles (48.28 km) per hour. Some witnesses put the speed at closer to 70 miles (112.65 km) per hour.

Regardless, Luciano's train was traveling at a speed far faster than was safe. Luciano would claim that he applied the brakes as he approached the fatal curve, but that they did not work. Later evidence clearly proved him wrong—the brakes were never administered.

As Luciano took the sharp tunnel curve, with a concrete barrier separating east and west tracks at the portal's entrance, his train left the tracks. The train, which consisted of three 32-year-old wooden cars and two steel cars, slammed into the concrete wall of the tunnel. One of every 7 of the train's 650 passengers was about to die.

CARNAGE

Exactly what happened during the next 10 seconds is open to conjecture. However, Brian Cudahy, in his exhaustive study, provided the most authoritative analysis when he wrote:

> The jolt of the derailment of the lead car disrupted the rhythms of the trailer cars, and both of them derailed before they reached the concrete tunnel portal. Each came in contact with the outside face of the portal before being dragged into the tunnel by the continuing force of the train's forward momentum. . . . The second trailer hooked the face of the portal squarely with its front corner. As it was then dragged forward into the tunnel, it was totally destroyed and would later be removed from the tunnel only as scrap and debris.

In the tunnel, the two derailed trailer cars suffered the most extensive carnage. Cudahy continued:

> Centrifugal force drove the two lightweight cars outward along and against the wall of the tunnel on the outside, or left side, of the entry curve. But the tunnel wall was not a flat or smooth surface; it was a structure whose vertical steel support columns extended out beyond the plane of the concrete wall itself, thus subjecting the cars to a horrible serration effect.

When the motormen working for the BRT went on strike, the subway company pushed inexperienced service workers into operating the train cars. This had devastating effects when an ill dispatcher was pushed into driving a train on an unfamiliar line. Without any previous knowledge of the sharp turns and s-curves (above) of the subway line, the motorman accidentally crashed his train into a wall, derailing two cars and causing almost 100 deaths.

Ninety-three people—most of them women—lost their lives, and more than a hundred were severely injured. One particular individual, though dazed and confused, was not physically hurt. Edward Luciano emerged from his motorman's cab, staggered around, boarded a trolley car, and went home. According to the *New York Times*, when detectives reached his home a few hours later, "Luciano was seated in a chair, pale as death. He was very nervous and seemed to be on the verge of a collapse." When he was asked what happened, all Luciano could say was, "I don't know. I lost control of the damn thing. That's all."

As many as 200 injured passengers were transported to nearby hospitals. Eight of the injured would die in the next couple of days, mostly from internal brain damage. Nearby Ebbets Field served as a temporary aid station for the less seriously hurt.

BUILDING AMERICA NOW

WASHINGTON METROPOLITAN AREA TRANSIT AUTHORITY (WMATA)

The Washington Metropolitan Area Transit Authority is said to operate the second-largest rail transit system in the United States, with a total of 106.3 miles (171 km) of service through 86 stations. Of that total, 50.5 miles (81.27 km) of track and 47 stations are used for its subway, considered by many to be the safest and cleanest in the country.

The final leg of the original WMATA rail network, which began operation in 1976, was completed in 2001. The authority services a 1,500-square-mile (3,885 sq km) area in which 3.5 million people live and work. It is estimated that 42 percent of those who work in the center of Washington, D.C., and parts of Arlington County, Virginia, use the mass-transit system. In fiscal year 2007, 207.9 million riders rode the WMATA rails, and another 131.5 million took its buses.

WMATA trains, which are some of the most modern in the world, are 75 feet (22.86 m) long and 10 feet (3 m) wide. They can travel up to 59 miles (95 km) per hour, although they average 33 miles (53.1 km) per hour, including stops. WMATA stations house 230 elevators and 588 escalators—including the one at Wheaton Station, which is said to be, at 230 feet (70.1 m), the longest escalator in the Western Hemisphere. One station, Forest Glen, is 196 feet (59.74 m) deep, or 21 stories into the ground.

According to Brian Cudahy, "Many later spoke in admiration of the efforts put forth by two unidentified sailors—passengers aboard the train—during the rescue effort. 'They seemed to have superhuman strength,' one rescue worker said. 'They worked for hours steadily, and then went away without telling who they were.'"

Once the living and the dead were removed from the scene, investigators descended to take photographs of the wreckage. The police department impounded the fatal train at the crash site and refused to let BRT officials near it. Evidence was needed for a possible criminal prosecution, which would begin almost immediately.

PLAYING POLITICS

Within 24 hours of the Malbone Street Wreck, as the November 1 disaster would forever be known, a full-blown formal proceeding got under way in a Flatbush magistrate's court in downtown Brooklyn. The presiding magistrate was none other than John Hylan, the mayor of New York City. Know as "Red Mike" because of his flaming red hair, the mayor—a former judge—had immediately invoked a little-known city charter provision that allowed him to declare himself a "committing magistrate." The mayor would be empowered to call witnesses, take testimony, and begin, as Brian Cudahy observed, "the task of establishing blame for the tragedy."

Why Hylan was so eager to take control and assign blame in the case is not difficult to understand. The mayor's zeal stemmed from two factors: a long-festering personal humiliation and a deep-seated personal conviction.

Hylan had, himself, been a motorman; he drove elevated steam-powered trains on the Brooklyn Union Elevated Railroad (part of the BRT) in 1897. In October of that year, Hylan was fired from his job for taking a curve too fast and almost striking his superintendent. Although Hylan denied being at fault—and claimed that, as a result of his actions, he actually saved his superintendent's life—the future mayor remained embittered by the dismissal for the rest of his life.

More significant, Hylan had developed over the years a real antipathy for privately run rapid transit. He believed that the public interest would be better served if mass transit were under municipal control—free of all distractions of profit and loss, and of corporate interests.

Clearly, as was seen when the investigative proceedings got under way, the mayor of New York had a distaste for the BRT. He wanted people punished—from Luciano at the bottom to the company officials at the top. Clear bias reined throughout the investigation. As Brian Cudahy noted in *The Malbone Street Wreck*, "So totally was he [Hylan] engulfed by a desire to embarrass higher officials of the BRT in the days and weeks after the accident, that his actions assumed a comic dimension and severely distorted the orderly quest for justice."

At the conclusion of Hylan's inquiry, on December 11, 1918, the mayor—acting as magistrate—declared that the crime of manslaughter had been committed and directed that six individuals be charged. Then, in a separate, more authoritative legal process, the grand jury handed down a series of criminal indictments against those six on December 19, 1918. One of the indicted was motorman Edward Luciano.

Luciano was in an interesting and unenviable position as the case went to trial. The BRT had hired a full battery of high-priced lawyers to defend all six of the accused, including Luciano. In so doing, Luciano was deprived of a defense that would have pitted him against the company. He thus could not lay blame on the BRT for the accident. Luciano would sink or swim with the indicted company officials. Five separate trials were conducted during a 13-month period (from March 1919 to January 1921), but the prosecution failed to obtain a single conviction.

In his defense, Luciano, carefully coached by BRT lawyers, described what he claimed to have done on the fateful night. "Then I started down toward the Consumers' Park station and expected to receive three bells to stop there," he said, as reported in the *New York Herald*. "None were rung. I shut off the power and started to coast. The train jumped ahead so fast that I put on the air [brakes], but they would not hold. Then I applied the emergency [brake], and that would not hold and I reversed my power. The next thing I knew we were crashing."

The BRT's own internal investigation later showed that Luciano did none of the things he described in court with regard to his actions just before the train crashed. He never applied any of the brakes. Had he possessed the skill to do so, the Malbone Street Wreck might never have occurred.

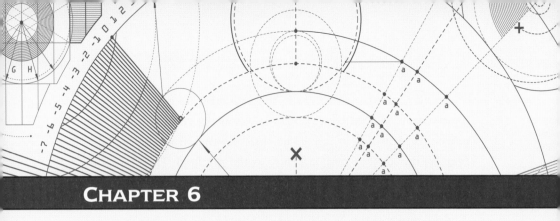

CHAPTER 6

Consolidation

The Malbone Street Wreck did not, in itself, force the Brooklyn Rapid Transit Company into bankruptcy. Although the BRT eventually paid $1.6 million in claims resulting from the tragedy, it was poor management and the BRT's weak revenue stream (the nickel fare) that forced it into receivership on January 1, 1919. In June 1923, a new entity, the Brooklyn-Manhattan Transit Company (BMT), acquired the assets of the BRT, refinanced its debt, and took over operations.

The IRT, by the end of World War I in 1918, was almost as close to insolvency as the BRT. From 1917 to 1921, its net income plunged by more than half, to approximately $4.5 million. Nonetheless, the IRT survived, battling postwar inflation, to limp through the Roaring Twenties.

Subway financial woes aside, use of New York's mass transit continued its upward climb in the 1920s, a decade known for spectacular economic growth. In 1913, New Yorkers averaged 161 subway rides annually. By 1925, the number had jumped to 276.

Much of New York City's economic boom centered on real estate development, most visibly with the huge skyscrapers going up in downtown and midtown Manhattan. The Chrysler Building, the Manhattan Building, and the Empire State Building, all constructed during the speculative boom, characterized the times.

Of course, skyscrapers needed tenants and customers. Buildings under construction in the late 1920s were expected to bring 180,000 people per day into Manhattan alone. To make that possible, the subway would have to handle the traffic. Together, skyscrapers and the subway worked to advance Manhattan's 1920's growth. The city's skyscrapers simply could not have been built had the subway not existed to supply the edifices with their daily workers and visitors.

As a result of the Dual Contracts, subway trackage now extended way beyond Manhattan Island, into the Bronx, Brooklyn, and Queens. Real estate developers once again took advantage.

One such developer was Edward Archibald MacDougall. By 1914, the enterprising MacDougall had acquired 350 acres of marshland in Flushing, Queens. Although it was originally called Trains Meadow, MacDougall soon renamed his plot of land Jackson Heights and dreamed of turning it into an upscale residential apartment complex. There was one major drawback, however: Jackson Heights was relatively inaccessible. For white-collar workers to get from Manhattan's business districts to Flushing was a time-consuming, transfer-plagued, and often street-level ordeal that would take well over an hour. Suburbanites would never be willing to suffer the ride.

All that changed, however, when the IRT, as part of its Dual Contracts expansion, announced a route that would take subway riders right to Jackson Heights and beyond. "Once the line to Jackson Heights opened on April 21, 1917, passengers could board an IRT train at the Eighty-second Street station—the twelfth stop in Queens—and arrive at Grand Central Terminal in twenty to twenty-five minutes," Clifton Hood reported. "Afterward, Queensboro's real estate ads regularly boasted that Jackson Heights was only a twenty-two-minute subway trip from Grand Central."

By 1919, Jackson Heights, recognized as the nation's first garden apartment suburb, was open and accepting residents. Because the complex was a cooperative, an individual actually purchased his or her own apartment and became a homeowner. By April 1921, 600 families had moved into

As New York City continued to grow, enormous construction projects for skyscrapers like the Chrysler Building (above) came to define a new era of wealth and prosperity for the metropolis. With real estate prices soaring, especially in Manhattan, the subway made it possible for people to live in less expensive neighborhoods and work in the heart of the city.

CHICAGO TRANSIT AUTHORITY AND THE LOOP

In October 1897, the 2-mile (3.2 km), double-track Union Loop elevated line in Chicago's Central District opened for service. Despite numerous attempts during the past century to eliminate the unsightly el and replace it with a subway system, Chicago's Loop has remained the heart of downtown mass transit. No major alterations have been made in the more than 100 years that the Loop has serviced the downtown Chicago business community. Although the Loop is considered by many to be ugly, noisy, awkward, and inhibiting of light, air, and street activity, it has become a Chicago institution. Every city transit plan has called for its removal—to no avail.

If opponents of the Loop ever had a chance to push forward a subway replacement plan, it came in 1977, when an extraordinary accident occurred: the Chicago Loop derailment. At 5:25 P.M. on February 4, a transit authority elevated train rear-ended another train. Cars fell off the elevated track to the street below. Eleven people were killed, and 183 were injured.

The tragic accident notwithstanding, the Loop has survived. Many residents insist on likening the Chicago Loop to San Francisco's cable cars. Chicago does have a subway, but its Loop will remain up and running for the foreseeable future.

the eight-building development. The new digs were decidedly upscale. According to Clifton Hood, "Jackson Heights achieved a high standard of apartment construction. It embellished the facades, stairways, and halls with ornate architectural details and provided parquet floors, fireplaces, sunrooms, built-in bathtubs with showers, and solid plaster construction in its flats."

SUBWAY ESCAPE

With just one nickel, a person could, in the 1920s, travel almost anywhere in the Greater New York City area. One might live in the Bronx—across from the recently constructed Yankee Stadium (1923)—and travel into Manhattan, over to Brooklyn, and down to the beach resorts in the far south for a total cost of five cents.

That New Yorkers took advantage of the relatively free recreational opportunity such a trip to the beach afforded is an understatement. "On a hot summer day in the 1920s it was not uncommon for Coney Island's attendance to top the million mark—and counting," noted Stan Fischler, author of *The Subway and the City: Celebrating a Century*. And why not? As Fischler continued, "Coney Island meant Steeplechase—The Funny Place; Wonder Wheel, The Bobsled, Faber's Poker, Feltman's Pavilion, Milo, the Mule-Faced Boy, Tirza and Her Wine Bath, and, of course, Nathan's Famous Hot Dogs, among other attractions." Coney Island had been established in 1878 as a middle-class playground. By the 1920s, when the new subway service became linked with the refurbished Brighton Surface line, the amusement park was accessible to all New Yorkers.

Recreation and the subway, like skyscrapers and the subway, had been relentlessly linked from the day the IRT line opened in 1904. Nowhere was this more apparent than with baseball parks and stadiums. Sites for both Ebbets Field in Brooklyn and Yankee Stadium in the Bronx were chosen with subway lines and stations as key determining factors. Without the subway to deposit tens of thousands of fans into the ballparks, neither facility could have been successful.

Ebbets Field, home of the Brooklyn Dodgers—so named because Brooklyn residents were always dodging surface streetcar traffic—first opened its turnstiles on April 9, 1913. The IRT to the north and the BRT to the west were either already in place or soon would be. Within a short time, the area around the baseball

Stadiums for New York's baseball teams were built based on their access to the subway. With the Dodgers located in Brooklyn and the Yankees playing in the Bronx, showdowns between the two teams soon became known as subway series. *Above,* Yankee Stadium during a World Series game between the Brooklyn Dodgers and the New York Yankees.

field experienced an economic boom and revitalization. According to Fischler, "The subway—and Ebbets Field—contributed to…the total revitalization of the neighborhood which, from Eastern Parkway south to Empire Boulevard, became known as Crown Heights."

Yankee Stadium, called "the House That Ruth Built" in honor of baseball superstar Babe Ruth, opened for play in 1923. To choose his site, owner Jacob Ruppert observed a simple dictum, as reported by Stan Fischler: "Just follow the new, growing subway." Eventually, baseball fans of both the Dodgers and the Yankees would travel back and forth between Ebbets Field and Yankee Stadium, in what was known as a subway series, when the teams played each other.

To move the masses and get them on the trains, the subway's rolling stock had to be constantly improved. Cars were originally composites of wood with a metal underframe. Soon, however, all-steel versions took hold. Had all five cars on the Malbone Street run of November 1, 1918, been made of metal instead of mostly wood, there is little doubt that fewer lives would have been lost.

In 1913, the BRT set in motion the purchase that would eventually amount to 950 new all-steel cars. This new car, known as the "Standard," came to be regarded as the finest and most durable piece of railway rolling stock in the world.

The Standard measured 67 feet (20.4 m) long, which was 16 feet (4.8 m) longer than anything on the IRT lines. Instead of doors in the end vestibules, the Standard had three sets of twin doors spaced along both sides of the car. The doors were electro-pneumatically operated by a conductor in the center of the car. By 1921, the system allowed one conductor to operate all of the doors on an eight-car train.

THE INDEPENDENT SUBWAY (IND)

New York mayor John Hylan's "defeat"—not getting the convictions he wanted in the Malbone Street Wreck indictments—only solidified his antipathy for subway operations in private hands. His Honor would dislike the IRT and the BRT (later the BMT) for the rest of his life.

Not that the two privately owned, Dual Contracts subways serving Greater New York City in the 1920s needed additional trouble. In an attempt to reign in costs, to counter the devastating postwar inflation of the 1920s and the stranglehold of the nickel fare, both companies thinned their workforces and took other cost-cutting actions. Between 1918 and 1928, the IRT, for example, reduced the number of employees per million car miles from 85 to 45. Both companies resorted to deferred maintenance, which limited the cleaning of platforms, toilets, and the cars themselves. According to Clifton Hood, "In 1927, IRT President Frank Hedley expressed the company's new approach by saying, 'I saw a car with clean windows today, and when I got back to the office I raised hell to find out who cleaned those windows and spent all that money.'"

Hylan thought that the answer to subway failure was simple: Place the IRT and the BMT in public hands. If that could not happen, the mayor wanted a new, additional subway, independent and under municipal control. In September 1922, the mayor published a report entitled *Mayor Hylan's Plan for Real Rapid Transit*, which, according to Clifton Hood, "argued that subways should be 'planned, built, and operated to accommodate the transportation needs of the people . . . and not solely for the financial advantage of the operating companies and their officials.'"

Three years later, on March 14, 1925, Mayor Hylan broke ground on the first leg of what was called the Independent Subway System, or IND. New York would get a third subway—one that was owned, constructed, and operated by the city—at an estimated cost of $674 million.

The IND had two main purposes. First, it would provide better, competing services in the business and residential districts of Manhattan. Second, it would replace the island's four elevateds with underground service. In total, seven new routes (including those into the outer boroughs) and approximately 190 additional track miles (305.7 km) were created.

The first route of the IND, the Eighth Avenue section, opened on September 10, 1932. The last, much delayed route, the Sixth Avenue section, opened on December 14, 1940. Building the new subway was, according to Croff Conklin, author of *All About Subways*, "one of the greatest engineering feats man has ever accomplished."

Vivian Heller, in *The City Beneath Us*, elaborated on Conklin's comment when he said of the IND's construction:

> The building of the IND was a gargantuan enterprise. Constructed piecemeal during the Great Depression, it took seven million man-hours to complete. Penetrating the most highly developed districts of New York, construction was never simple or straightforward. By the time it was finished in 1940, 26 miles of water and gas pipes, 350 miles of electrical conduits, and 18 miles of sewers had been rerouted.

Although the IND provided additional track mileage (something Manhattan had an insatiable demand for) and the island's four detested els eventually came down, the city had taken on a huge new burden in building and operating the IND. The system, which was never profitable, ran up large deficits from the beginning. As one financial expert declared, as quoted by Vivian Heller, "The City didn't get what it paid for although it certainly paid for what it got."

UNIFICATION (IRT, BMT, IND)

The Great Depression of the 1930s devastated the New York economy. In 1930, the Depression's first full year, unemployment in the city quadrupled. By year's end, 6,000 people sold apples on street corners, crouching, in the words of Gene Folwer, "like 'half-remembered sins . . . on the conscience of the town.' " Soon, one of every six New Yorkers was out of work. In Harlem, it was one of every four.

Because far fewer people were working, not as many commuters rode the subway. As the Depression worsened, the nickel fare became prohibitive for some people. Clifton Hood cited a couple who—although they were employed—survived by economizing to the extreme. "They regarded the five-cent subway fare an unaffordable luxury and often walked 40 or 50 blocks [approximately

2–3 miles] from their apartment on West 107th Street in Manhattan to avoid paying for the IRT."

In Depression-time New York, it was no surprise that the IND suffered financially. According to Vivian Heller, "The city was paying nine cents on every nickel ride at a time when the true cost of a single ride was fourteen cents." The year the IND first opened, 1932, the IRT went into receivership. The BMT stayed solvent throughout the 1930s, but barely. Vivian Heller declared, "Starved of capital, its equipment breaking down, the transit industry was suffering."

Riders felt the decline with a visible deterioration in service. "The subways were dirty and unattractive," declared Clifton Hood. "Station benches that had once been painted bright yellow were now worn, chipped, and greasy, while the platforms were often covered with peanut shells, banana skins, candy wrappers, and old newspapers. The trains were old and drab. During the Depression, the subways were flooded with homeless people who slept or panhandled there."

On January 1, 1934, New York City installed its ninety-ninth mayor—the plump, multilingual Fiorello H. LaGuardia. He became New York's chief executive in what many consider the bleakest moment in the city's history.

When it came to the subway, LaGuardia was committed to two unshakable principles: the nickel fare and the unification of New York's rapid transit—all of it. To the mayor and his supporters, the subway was in a state of crisis that demanded a complete restructuring.

Following the signing of the Dual Contracts in 1913, the city of New York was expecting to reap large revenues from expanded ridership. By the late 1930s, however, the city had received nothing from the BRT, and only $19 million from the IRT. By combining the management of the IRT, the BRT, and the IND, the reasoning went, the city would save millions of dollars through an efficiency of scale.

In late 1939, the parties came to an agreement. The city would purchase the BMT subway, els, trolleys, and buses for $175 million. It would acquire IRT assets for $151 million. With its 500 rapid-transit stations and 760 miles (1,223 km) of track, the unification deal, which was signed on December 12, 1939, became the largest railroad merger in U.S. history.

SUBWAY TOKEN:
Good for a Ride

When the New York Subway fare increased from 10 cents to 15 cents in 1953, the system faced a major problem: Turnstiles could not handle two coins (a dime and a nickel). As a result, subway officials created the first full-fare token, worth 15 cents and designed to fit into the dime-accepting turnstiles. The tokens, 48 million of which were minted between 1953 and 1970, contained a distinctive Y-shaped hole and stayed in circulation even when the price for a subway ride was raised to 20 cents in 1966.

A larger "Y" token, 50 million of which would eventually be minted, appeared in 1970, when the subway fare increased to 30 cents. When the fare reached 50 cents a ride in 1980, the token was still in circulation.

To celebrate the subway's Diamond Jubilee in 1979, 5.8 million better-looking tokens—with a small, diamond-shaped hole—were minted. A message at the top read "People Moving People." Between 1980 and 1985, 60 million brass tokens were minted. The dollar "bullseye" token appeared in 1986 and stayed in use until 1995. It achieved a total mintage of 90 million.

The last token issued by the Metropolitan Transit Authority—a token known as the "Five Boroughs"—was placed into service in 1995. The previous year, the subway had issued its first MetroCard. Tokens were taken out of circulation in May 2003, one year before the subway's hundredth anniversary.

The subway's transition from private to municipal owner-ship was ironic. As Brian Cudahy observed of the paradox, with regard to the Dual Contracts partners, "Their status as profit-seeking corporations was a liability in 1940; it had been a salvation in 1913."

MASS TRANSIT AND THE AUTOMOBILE

Various commuter irritations aside, the 1920s and 1930s were a good time to ride the subway in New York City. For the pal-try nickel fare, commuters and sightseers alike could travel around Manhattan, into the boroughs, and to seaside resorts, and they could do it night or day, seven days a week. The sub-way had become the "people's subway"; young and old, rich and poor, laborers and Wall Street brokers shared the seats and the straps. The subway, with all of its "color," somehow repre-sented the "truth" about New York, said essayist Christopher Morley.

In the third and fourth decades of the twentieth century, the New York Subway was often considered cheap, reliable, acces-sible, and, above all, safe. Although the subway may have been uncomfortable and grimy, it was never dangerous in the way it would be a few decades later. As the *New York Times* declared, "In the lexicon of the New York City subway, the term 'safety' referred to train accidents and collisions, not crime."

Although ridership dipped in the Depression decade of the 1930s, from a high of 2 billion in 1930 to 1.8 billion in 1940, it rose again during the four years of World War II (1941–1945). "There was a six-day workweek, which meant you had people taking the subway an extra day a week, and there were very few automo-biles," noted Jim Dwyer, in *Subway Lives: 24 Hours in the Life of the New York Subway.* "On December 23, 1946, the all-time record for passengers was set when 8,872,244 riders were carried in a twenty-four-hour period." In the early 1940s, the New York Transit System actually earned a profit.

Because more people relied on the subway for professional and recreational purposes, an upgrade was needed to meet the increased demand for transportation. New steel cars featuring more doors and better technology were introduced to the public in 1913, improving the subway experience for its riders. *Above*, passengers in 1933 board a steel car on the city's newly extended Eighth Avenue subway.

That profit evaporated in 1947, when the unified system incurred an operating deficit of $18 million—its first loss. The New York Subway would never again be profitable.

If one factor, above all else, contributed to a decline of subway usage in the post–World War II decade, it was the rise of the automobile. The building of freeways and expressways was a national trend, and the rush to the suburbs, especially to Long Island, was an inescapable fact of New York living in the 1940s and 1950s. Although the subway provided a mode of transportation to get people in and out of the working city, it was the automobile—speeding along new multilane highways—that most commuters now chose.

The man most responsible for accelerating the auto trend was Robert Moses, a "master builder" and genius of twentieth-century urban planning. Moses, a true visionary, was said to care more about cars than he did about people. This observation, although probably true, was even more ironic because, in his long life (1888–1981), the all-powerful public-works czar never learned to drive.

At one point, Moses held no fewer than 12 separate titles; he had four opulent offices across the city and in Long Island. As Vivian Heller observed of Moses, "Preserving the character of old buildings and neighborhoods was far less important to him than providing scenic 'ribbon parks' that could be admired in passing, from the windows of a speeding car. With a brilliance matched by burning ambition, Moses dominated New York's bridges, tunnels, and roadways for almost fifty years."

In the end, Moses's 627 miles of highway (built between 1945 and 1970) became hopelessly clogged with backed-up cars. There simply could never be enough express lanes to get people in and out of Manhattan. As the twentieth century crossed its halfway mark and raced into the 1960s and 1970s, New Yorkers, it turned out, needed their subway more than ever.

CHAPTER 7

Nervous Breakdown

The nickel of 1904 had, four decades later, lost more than half its value. The New York Subway system should have been charging its riders 11 cents a trip as the mid-century approached, but it was still collecting only a nickel. For the subway to survive, to achieve some sort of long-term fiscal sanity, the price of a ride would have to go up. In 1948, it finally did.

In 1904, when the subway first opened for business, a rider bought a ticket the same way someone purchases a movie ticket a century later. A passenger approached a wooden ticket booth, handed over a nickel, and received a paper ticket. The rider would then proceed to a ticket chopper—an individual who would, with the use of an enclosed mini-guillotine, chop the ticket in half. The passenger was then permitted to board a subway train.

By 1920, with labor costs rising, August Belmont had his engineers design an automatic turnstile that would accept the nickel coin directly. As a result, more than a thousand ticket choppers lost their jobs. The subway, however, saved a bundle. Invention of the turnstile is considered by some to have been the greatest technological advance of the decade.

With the Second World War over, and increased ridership threatened by the rise of the automobile, clamor to increase the subway fare reached a fever pitch. Once thought of as political suicide, raising the fare after the war became an operational necessity. Paul Windels, a conservative businessman with impeccable integrity and a brilliant mind, led the charge to raise the fare. As head of the "Committee of Fifteen," a civic group that advocated reduced municipal expenditures, Windels was quick to cite a 1943 survey showing that, of the country's 25 largest cities, only New York retained the nickel fare.

Windels wanted to double the subway fare to a dime. "Isn't it worth the difference," he asked a radio audience in 1943, as reported by Clifton Hood, "to pay an honest fare instead of a political fare and get decent service instead of the poor service we're getting today?"

Opposition to a fare increase remained widespread. A coalition of liberals, socialists, and communists, along with many labor leaders, were dead set against any increase. They feared it would hurt the poor and the working class. Initially, the Transport Workers Union (TWU) was opposed, too. Their wages had gone up by 27 percent from 1941 to 1945; however, it was now 1948, and if subway revenue continued to decline, the union reasoned, wages would surely follow.

When Mike Quill, the TWU's combative Irish-born president, announced in March 1948 that he was in favor of the 10-cent fare—telling the union rank and file that it would increase their wages—a deal was assured. New York City mayor William O'Dwyer announced on April 20, 1948, that the fare would rise to 10 cents. On July 1, 44 years after the subway took in its first nickel, riders began to pay a dime to ride the rails. In five years, the fare would rise again, to 15 cents. By the subway's one-hundredth anniversary, in 2004, the fare had climbed to $2.

Automatic turnstiles directly accepting nickels made ticket choppers obsolete. As the subway began to grow and fares started to rise, turnstiles needed to be upgraded to meet these changes. When additional fare increases threatened the efficiency of these new turnstiles, the subway token was introduced to the public.

TRANSIT STRIKE

As the price of a subway ticket rose in the 1950s and 1960s, so did the economic woes of New York City. The Big Apple, once a thriving manufacturing center with employment that supported generations of immigrants, saw many jobs flee to outlying areas in the post–World War II era. So, too, did middle-class residents, who headed for the suburbs and—instead of mass transit—often traveled the ribbon of new highways snaking through the outer boroughs. Along with these changes, public transit workers had won the right to unionize. If they could unionize, they could strike—and strike they did.

It happened on New Year's Day of 1966, the day newly elected mayor John Lindsay took office. For the mayor, it was a rough beginning. For New Yorkers who would have to endure the complete shutdown of mass transit, it was even worse.

"We want half-pay pensions after 25 years of service, regardless of age," Michael Quill, the still fiery head of the Transport Workers Union declared in November 1965, as reported by Vivian Heller. "We want six weeks of vacation after one year of service." When a reporter responded to Quill's demand with, "Why not ask for a paid vacation on the Rivera?" the union boss quipped, "That's not for this strike, that's for the next. We want a four-day, 32-hour work week with no loss of pay—and we're going to get it, too."

At 5:00 P.M. on January 1, 1966, 34,000 transit workers walked off the job, shutting down the entire subway system and all bus lines for the first time in New York's history. By the second day of the strike, car-clogged roads leading into Manhattan were at a standstill, and commuters were stranded in an attempt to get to work. New York City was completely shut down.

Although the TWU immediately reduced its salary demands, the Transit Authority (TA), the agency that now ran mass transit in New York, responded by getting a judge's order for the arrest of Quill and eight other union leaders. "The judge can drop dead in his black robes," Quill responded, as quoted by Vivian Heller. "I don't care if I rot in jail, I will not call off this strike."

Quill did not, however, rot in jail. Two hours after he arrived at the local prison, Quill—who was not in good health to begin with—suffered congestive heart failure. He was immediately transferred to Bellevue Hospital and later to Mt. Sinai Medical Hospital.

The strike continued as the city was tied up in knots. According to Vivian Heller, "Although no one was allowed to visit Quill [in the hospital], Richard Price, a close adviser to the mayor, was finally admitted into his room. The attending doctor removed Quill's oxygen tank just long enough for the sick man to hold up four fingers—indicating that the strike would end when a four-day workweek was obtained."

On January 13, one of the most prolonged mass-transit strikes in U.S. history ended. The union averaged pay gains of 9 percent for the next eight years, along with increased pension benefits and additional paid holidays.

Quill, who was released from the hospital on January 25, had little time to enjoy what most observers agreed was a clear union

MIXED REVIEWS:
The Subway in Film

The New York Subway has been depicted in dozens of movies since its own debut in 1904. In some cases, it has made a strictly cameo appearance. In others, the subway has been cast as the central character. Either way, the underground railway is portrayed either as relatively benign or, in several films, as a representation of the decay and mayhem that inflicted New York City at the time. Following are a few of the more notable early films, all worth renting:

★ *Speedy* (1928) is a silent film that stars comedian Harold Lloyd. It includes a fun tour of the city, introducing the viewer to Coney Island, Yankee Stadium, and the incomparable Babe Ruth.

★ *King Kong* (1933) is, to be sure, famous far more for its Empire State Building scenes than the giant ape's tearing up of the Third Avenue el. That said, for a good representation of the base intrusion that els inflicted on New York, this movie cannot be beat.

★ *Lost Weekend* (1945) tells the story of an alcoholic, with the local el as backdrop. One cannot miss the connection victory. The TWU leader, head of the union from its inception in the 1930s, died on January 28. Four days later, 3,000 transit workers filed past Quill's casket at St. Patrick's Cathedral to pay their last respects.

GRAFFITI BLIGHT

At first, transit workers who saw it were stymied, as were subway riders who happened to notice. In 1970, the cryptic scrawl "TAKI 183" appeared all over station walls and subway cars. Maybe it was a surveyor's mark, or perhaps a maintenance designation?

between the intrusive el and the poverty of surrounding neighborhoods.

★ *On the Town* (1949) tells the story of three happy-go-lucky sailors out to explore New York City, where "the people ride in a hole in the ground."

★ *The French Connection* (1971) is all about city and subway, mayhem, menace, noise, and dirt, with a great car chase under an overhead el.

★ *Death Wish* (1972), which stars Charles Bronson, was the beginning of a series of vigilante films designed, most effectively, to feed on riders' revenge fantasies.

★ *The Taking of Pelham 1-2-3* (1974) depicts the actual hijacking of a subway train.

Many films made as late as the early 1980s chose to show the subway as a place of, as Michael Brooks noted, "sneering villains, flying bullets, and fiery explosions." Yet, the fact that more recent films tend to downplay such carnage—or fail to depict it at all—is perhaps testimony to a changing perception, as well as the reality, of the New York Subway in the twenty-first century.

Actually, what more than a few people had begun to notice was the beginning of something new to the times—something that would grow, like ooze in a science-fiction movie, to cover a myriad of city surfaces. It was graffiti, 1970's style.

TAKI 183 was Demetrius, a Greek-American kid from Washington Heights who was employed part-time as a messenger. He rode the subway from one part of New York City to the other, delivering packages and envelopes. (Taki was his nickname; 183 the street he lived on.) Demetrius told the *New York Times* why he wrote TAKI 183 everywhere he could, as quoted by Jim Dwyer:

> "I didn't have a job then, and you pass the time, you know," he said. "I just did it everywhere I went. You don't do it for the girls, they don't seem to care. You do it for yourself. You don't go after it to be elected president.... I don't feel like a celebrity normally. But the guys make me feel like one when they introduce me to someone. 'This is him,' they say. The guys know who the first one was."

Graffiti in itself was not new; the Roman authorities had to deal with it, as did IRT officials the day the subway opened in 1904. Still, what took off in the early 1970s and exploded in the 1980s was different, if only in its pervasiveness. It was everywhere; in some subway cars it covered every inch, inside and out. Taggers took to writing on top of others' "art" because there was no blank space left.

To a few, graffiti was indeed art—a new form of urban expression. "At its best, graffiti brought surprise to a ride that had seemed the foundation of the daily grind," Michael Brooks observed. "The city offered few sights more remarkable than the view of the intersecting el tracks near East Tremont Avenue at West Farms Plaza where the Bronx River flowed in the foreground while two trains, their entire surfaces painted in bold forms and bright colors, passed overhead."

robbing Goetz. Goetz, however, sensed an aggressive and threatening manner in Canty and his three comrades, and he became defensive. When Canty repeated his request, Goetz told investigators later, as reported in the *New York Times*, "I snapped." His intention at that instant was to "murder them, to hurt them, to make them suffer as much as possible."

BUILDING AMERICA NOW

SOUTHEASTERN PENNSYLVANIA TRANSPORTATION AUTHORITY (SEPTA)

The Southeastern Pennsylvania Transportation Authority, established in 1964 and based in Philadelphia, services 3.8 million people in a 2,200-square-mile (5,698 sq km), five-county area. It is one of only two multimodal transit operations in the United States. As such, SEPTA provides its constituency with bus, subway, elevated rail, regional rail, light rail, and electric trolley services. It is the fifth-largest transit system in the United States. SEPTA has 280 active stations, more than 450 miles (724 km) of track, and a paying ridership of close to 307 million people annually. On a given workday, 1 million people ride a SEPTA vehicle.

Philadelphia was one of the first cities in the United States to build a subway, opening its Market Street Subway–Elevated line on April 6, 1907. Service was mainly on elevated track; the trains went "underground" only when they entered a short tunnel through the city center. Twenty-one years later, in 1928, the Broad Street Subway was added to the system, and in 1932, the Ridge Avenue–Eighth Street spur was completed.

Today, SEPTA operates two subway–elevated lines, using 343 vehicles, through 52 stations. Below ground, on the ground, and above ground, SEPTA is a truly mixed-transit urban system.

After years of deferred maintenance and neglect, the subway was inundated with incidents of crime and vandalism. In 1984, subway violence made headlines when electrical engineer Bernard Goetz *(in handcuffs)* shot four young men he believed intended to rob him on the subway.

What happened next took less than 1.6 seconds. Drawing his .38 caliber gun, Goetz fired five shots in rapid succession. He hit all four of the men, and Canty twice. "If I had more bullets, I would have shot them again, and again, and again," Goetz confessed later. Although all four men survived, one (named Darrell Cabey) was permanently paralyzed and suffered brain damage when a bullet severed his spine.

Public reaction was immediate, intense, and polarizing. Goetz was dubbed the "Subway Vigilante" by the press. Some people saw Goetz as a hero who stood up to crime and violence—particularly that perpetrated by young adults, and particularly by black men. Novelist Wesley Brown summed up the suspicions and fears of many New Yorkers when he declared, as quoted by Michael Brooks, "a display of bravado by a young, indigo-skinned black male, moving through a crowded subway car like a point guard bringing the ball up the court, sporting a haircut that makes the shape of his head resemble a cone of ice-cream, and wearing barge-sized sneakers with untied laces thick as egg noodles, is immediately considered a dangerous presence whether he is or not."

Others viewed Goetz's shooting as callous, an overreaction to what was a disturbing bit of panhandling but nothing more. The Reverend Al Sharpton called Goetz's actions racist.

At the criminal trial, Goetz claimed self-defense. He was, nonetheless, convicted of criminal possession of a weapon in the third degree and eventually served an eight-month prison sentence. In a subsequent civil trail, an all-black jury awarded Cabey $43 million. Goetz filed for bankruptcy.

Regardless of how New Yorkers viewed the outcome of both trials, there is little question that what happened on the subway in late December 1984 reflected growing frustration with the system's inability to control crime and degradation. As Michael Brooks declared, "By 1987 [hell] no longer seemed like a meta-phor at all. The decline in the city was real, the graffiti on the cars was real, and Bernard Goetz in his statements to the police sounded like nothing so much as one of the dammed."

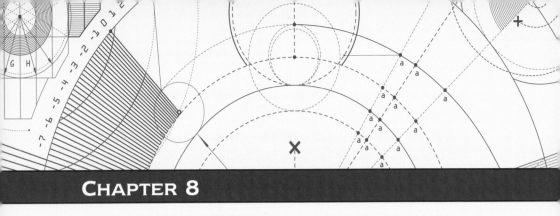

CHAPTER 8

Subway Renaissance

On April 1, 1980, it happened again: The Transport Workers Union (TWU) called a strike, yanking 34,000 New York subway and bus employees off the job. This strike—the second in the union's history—lasted 11 days, just one day short of the 1966 strike. The new strike would be even more disruptive than the first.

By law, however, it shouldn't have happened. In response to the 1966 transit work stoppage, the state of New York had passed the Taylor Law, which, among other things, prohibited public employees from striking. The law compelled the parties—in the case of transit, the Metropolitan Transit Authority (MTA) and the TWU—to submit to binding arbitration in the event of an impasse in their negotiations. If the union chose to strike anyway, it would be fined severely. The union did strike, and a fine was imposed.

The effect on New York and its commuters was devastating. All subway and bus lines in the city's five boroughs were brought to a complete standstill. The private sector lost an estimated

$100 million a day as a result of the walkout. Employee absenteeism reached 20 percent.

In an attempt to deal with what was sure to be massive daily traffic surges into Manhattan, the city implemented mandatory carpooling. Any car that entered the city during rush hour had to carry at least three passengers.

Interestingly, the population of Manhattan actually grew during the strike; 500,000 workers chose to stay in local hotels. The number of those who commuted by bicycle was estimated to have increased by 200,000.

On April 11, the strike ended. The TWU won a 9 percent raise and increased cost-of-living adjustments. In response to the settlement, the MTA raised the price of a subway ride to 60 cents. Somebody had to pay for the workers' gains, and it would be the commuting public.

With this fare increase came a new token. Sixty million of the solid brass, coin-like mini-discs were minted beginning on June 28, 1980. The same token stayed in use as the fare moved to 75 cents in 1981, to 90 cents in 1984, and to one dollar in 1986. The nickel fare, which ended in 1948, was just a memory.

Although the 1980s began with subway breakdown, they ended with considerable growth. According to Mark Feinman:

> The 1980s could be summarized as the "Jekyll and Hyde" period of the New York subway system. As the decade began, it had the filthiest trains, the craziest graffiti, the noisiest wheels, and the weirdest passengers. By the end of the decade, it had cleaner trains, no graffiti, quieter wheels—and the weirdest passengers. (Okay, three out of four ain't bad.)

In late 1979, the MTA got a new director, Richard Ravitch. He immediately inherited a $200 million deficit. To raise revenue, New York governor Hugh Carey proposed charging area owners of automobiles and other vehicles a "user fee." It never happened.

A widespread transit workers' strike in 1980 saw 34,000 workers walk off the job when labor negotiations stalled between the workers' union and the MTA. Thousands of commuters were forced to carpool or walk to work *(above)*. By the end of the strike, the MTA was left with an enormous operating deficit and millions of subway and bus riders were subjected to a fare hike.

What took place instead was the elimination of the special half-fare program for the elderly during peak hours, along with the Sunday half-fare program for all riders. Although hundreds protested the program's elimination by the MTA, the agency saved $44 million.

Such savings aside, the Metropolitan Transit Authority would need the infusion of a lot more money. It would require billions, not millions, of dollars to turn New York transit around and make it a viable enterprise. As the decade progressed, those billions started to pour in.

BIG BUCKS TO SPEND

The commuter fare alone, no matter what it was, would never be enough to cover subway operating expenses. The New York Subway system, like mass transit in other urban areas, is staffed—both in people and equipment—based on peak, rush-hour needs. Although such rush-hour traffic has, from day one, taxed New York's subway system, off-peak hours see a distinct drop in ridership. (On a typical workday, the subway's people-per-car load reaches 85 between 7:00 A.M. and 8:00 A.M. but drops to 38 between 11:00 A.M. and noon.) Still, the Transit Authority must staff for maximum peak-time usage. Brian Cudahy summarized the dilemma as follows:

> Called peaking, by transit planners and operators . . . the cost of maintaining and operating a transit system is driven by the equipment and the facilities and the employees needed at the peak hours of service. That these resources remain idle, or underutilized, for 20 of the day's 24 hours underscores why private companies have fled from the transit scene and left the responsibility to the public sector, where corporate standards of efficiency and return on investment need not apply.

When it comes to financial need, just a little more than 50 percent of the New York Subway's routine operating expenses are met by paying passengers. The rest must come from subsidies supplied by various levels of government. New York City and state resources are a factor in supplying subsidized funding, but it became apparent as early as the 1960s that federal dollars would be needed both to sustain subway operation and to provide for capital improvements.

To that end, in 1981, MTA director Ravitch was able to secure $8.1 billion in funding from various government sources to upgrade New York's subway system. Reconstruction work began at the system's two main storage yards, one at 207th

Street in Manhattan and the other at the sprawling Coney Island facility. Contracts were let for $150 million in track, switch, and signal work, and subway station renovation began. In all,

BUILDING AMERICA NOW

MIAMI-DADE TRANSIT (MDT)

The Miami-Dade Transit system, created in 1960, is the fourteenth-largest public-transit operation in the United States. It is a four-mode system—Metrobus, Metrorail, Metromover, and Paratransit—used by 300,000 passengers daily. Two of the four modes, the Metromover and Paratransit, deserve special attention.

With regard to the Metromover, visions of Alfred Speer's 1874 Endless Railway Train proposal for New York come to mind. According to the Miami-Dade Transit Web site (http://www.miamidade.gov/transit):

> The electrically powered, fully automated people-mover system connects with Metrorail at Government Center and Brickell stations and with Metrobus at various locations throughout downtown Miami. Metromover offers convenient access to a variety of government, business, entertainment, and cultural centers in the central downtown, Omni, and Brickell areas.

Opened on April 17, 1986, the Metromover covers 1.9 miles (3 km) in an elevated double loop. In 2005, nearly 9 million people chose the Metromover to get them around the central business district. The loop runs from 5:00 A.M. to midnight seven day a week.

The MDT's Paratransit service, known as Special Transportation Service (STS), was established in 1976 to meet the needs of disabled citizens. Privately contracted sedans, vans, and van equipment with lifts provide door-to-door service for eligible customers. Service is offered with no restrictions on trip purpose.

every mile of main-line track was rebuilt, and 56 stations were rehabilitated.

It was the massive purchase of new stainless-steel subway cars—begun in 1982—that got the most notice, however. Here, the traveling public could see firsthand where the money was being spent. Known as Silverliners, and designated R-62s for the IRT line and R-68s for the BMT/IND division, these cars—purchased from overseas suppliers—were, for the most part, single units with full-width operator's cabs on each end. Nearly 2,000 of the new cars were bought. All were air-conditioned. They were definitely cleaner and more comfortable than anything ever before placed on subway tracks, and they were more efficient. The mean distance between failures (MDBF) climbed to 30,000 miles (48,280 km)—a considerable improvement over previous numbers.

The Silverliners were supposedly automated, which meant they should have provided nearly hands-off operation. Yet, according to Brian Cudahy, such automation was an illusion. "There was nothing about the R-62 and R-68 that resembles automated rapid transit at all," he wrote. "George Morris [the motorman who let Mayor George McClellan joyride the first subway train in 1904] would probably have no difficulty at all running an R-62!"

Jim Dwyer, writing in *Subway Lives*, was even more circumspect. He provided faint praise when he declared,

> With gleaming aluminum skins, air conditioning, comfortable seats, the R-68 cars were the equivalent of the dumb blond: Handsome in the extreme, mechanically scatterbrained. They were prone to starting without anyone in the driver's seat. . . . One time a train of R-68s pulled out of a station with a babystroller—and baby—jammed between the doors because all the alert systems for the train crew had failed.

Of the 6,318 new and refurbished cars owned by the MTA in the late 1980s, 19 percent were unavailable for use. Twelve hundred cars—$1.2 billion in rolling stock—were sitting in the MTA's 18 maintenance yards.

GRAFFITI CLEANUP

The image of 1,200 cars stacked up and idling in yards is a bit deceiving, however. Not all had experienced mechanical failure. Many were simply too ugly to move out. David Gunn, who took over as president of the Transit Authority in 1984, was content to let such cars sit, at least for a while. None, he insisted, would be allowed to leave the yards unless they were spotless. For Gunn, that meant graffiti-free.

By the early 1980s, the graffiti problem—for New York City as a whole and the subway in particular—had reached alarming proportions. In response, New York mayor Ed Koch called for dogs to "attack" the problem: He proposed that subway storage yards be surrounded by a fenced perimeter patrolled by unescorted guard dogs. Actually, the mayor went one step further. "If I had my way, I wouldn't put in dogs, but wolves," the mayor told the *New York Times*.

David Gunn had a better idea—one that saw 86 percent of the 5,956 subway cars rendered graffiti-free by 1988. The number of graffiti vandalism arrests would drop, according to the *New York Times*, from about 2,400 in 1984 to 1,900 in 1985, 1,000 in 1986, and only 300 in 1987.

The transit leader's success in all but erasing graffiti from transit property rests in his genius for figuring out what writing on walls and surfaces, particularly moving surfaces, was really all about. According to Vivian Heller:

> Gunn understood that a graffiti writer's chief thrill was to see his tag circulating through the city. Short-circuit this thrill, and the temptation would be gone—this was the principle of his Clean Car Campaign. No train would be allowed to leave the yard if it had graffiti, a policy that is still in place today, and any car discovered with graffiti had to be taken out of service within 24 hours.

One of the biggest improvements to the New York City Subway system was the introduction of new subway cars. Made of stainless steel, these new Silverliners *(above)* were sleek, modern, clean, comfortable, and equipped with air-conditioning.

"Public transport is a perfect target, over five million passengers pass through the stations each day; countless others observe the cars that travel above ground," noted the Department of Transport in its *Case Study Report on Graffiti.* "In order to remove the reward and hence the motivation, it is vital to clean off or cover over any graffiti before it can have an audience."

About 1,000 workers were hired to clean up the graffiti. "Initially, it was labor intensive," David Gunn told Constance Hays of the *New York Times.* "But once you get on top of it, it's not that big a deal to keep them clean."

"Some of the graffiti-free trains came from new cars being put into service, others from cars that were refurbished at the 207th

Street overhaul shop in upper Manhattan," Fox Butterfield wrote in the *New York Times*. "There, behind a 15-foot-high fence topped by coils of razor-ribbon wire and patrolled by dogs, the besmirched cars are stripped down, sanded and repainted. Lined up on tracks, they resemble circus trains painted by mad clowns."

By 1989, subway graffiti, at least the painted version, was a thing of the past. Yet early in the twenty-first century, the *New York Times* reported a new graffiti phenomenon—"scratchitti," in which tags are acid-etched into subway windows. According to Thomas Lueck, "Raising the specter of the bad old days, transit officials are vowing to fight a problem they say is even more menacing than the graffiti of decades past."

RIDING THE MTA

William Barclay Parsons, the IRT's chief engineer, was invited to offer his thoughts on the state of his creation on the subway's twenty-fifth anniversary in 1929. Writing in the *New York Times*, as quoted by Brian Cudahy, Parsons declared, "As a matter of fact, New York was the first city in the world to develop a transit problem; since then it has never been without one, and it bids fair to retain one indefinitely." Given the system's growing complexity, could it ever be otherwise?

When, in 1982, subway maintenance crews sought to refurbish subway stations, they came across a curious problem at the 51st Street–Lexington Avenue station. The one-year-old floor tiles were popping up, many of them having been chipped away by women's high heels. The glue that held the tiles in place was no good. Before the tiles were laid, the 51st Street station, like most in the system, had had to settle for cement floors. The floors, over the years, came to take on what Jim Dwyer called a "chewing gum motif." Even when attacked with high-pressure sprays, special solvents, and quick freezes, the gum was a nightmare to remove. Finally, one subway rider, Barry Meier, pondered the two problems—that of keeping tile down and getting gum up.

According to Dwyer, Meier asked, "Why not use chewing gum to hold the tiles?"

As the twentieth century ended, New York was being flooded with immigrants—not from eastern and southern Europe but from Asia, the Caribbean, and Central America. The city's subway riders reflected the change. Although some people—such as conservative writer Peter Brimelow—saw the development as, in dark, hellish terms, "an underworld that is almost entirely colored" (as quoted by Michael Brooks), many saw a multiracial city worth celebrating. "On the subway," Xin Han, an immigrant from the People's Republic of China, declared, "we see the whole structure—happiness, hate, isolation and the desire for the American ideal."

Jim Dwyer was quick to see the subway's passenger diversity reflected in those who ran and maintained the system as well. With more than half of New York transit workers coming from Ireland well into the 1940s, the Transport Workers Union was shocked when it woke one day, in 1985, to find it had chosen a president not born on the Emerald Island. "Today, Dwyer observed, "the ascension of a black middle class can be gauged by watching the faces in the token booths, the conductor's cabs, or behind the windshield of the train operators' cars. . . . Today, there may be a sprinkling of Irish-born subway workers, but by far the largest group is American-born blacks. . . . They have their chance at the American dream because they went down to climb up."

Racial and ethnic makeup aside, the Transport Workers Union was unchanged in some respects as the twenty-first century dawned. On December 20, 2005, the union struck for the third time. When the union was fined $1 million a day for each day it kept the system down, and each worker was docked two days' pay for every day missed, settlement was reached—or, some would say, imposed—in just three days. Two days before Christmas, the subway trains and buses were rolling again. The New York Subway was 101 years old and counting.

SUBWAY RENAISSANCE

The year was 2004. New York's mayor, Michael Bloomberg, was there, of course, as had been his predecessor, George McClellan, in 1904. So, too, were the highest-level transit agency employees. Regular subway workers were dressed in period costume, and a barbershop quartet sang vintage songs. It was the start of the centennial celebrations, a time to mark the hundredth anniversary of New York City's crowning achievement, its subway system.

THE WORLD'S LARGEST ART MUSEUM:
Arts for Transit

Art has been a part of the New York Subway system since construction began in 1900. "From the beginning, the New York subway's creators never thought of the project solely as a means of transportation," said Joseph Giovannini in the introduction to *Subway Style: 100 Years of Architecture & Design in the New York City Subway*, published by the New York Transit Museum:

> Conceived in the 1890s and brought to fruition at the height of the newly fashionable City Beautiful movement, the subway was viewed as a major urban design program. . . . This attention to and respect for a functional yet beautiful subway system continued throughout the twentieth century, leading the evolution of subway design to mirror the world of art and architecture as these struggled between traditional European models and more modernist expression of industrial technology.

Today, this tradition continues, primarily through the work of the MTA's Arts for Transit program. The purpose of the program is to "encourage the use of public transit by presenting visual and performing arts projects in subway and commuter rail stations."

The original City Hall station, out of service since 1945, was spruced up and reopened for the occasion. Just as Mayor McClellan had done on opening day, October 27, 1904, Mayor Bloomberg took control of a subway train (this one with five fully restored IRT cars) and drove it out of the station. New Yorkers had much to celebrate in marking their subway's one-hundredth birthday.

The statistics were mind-boggling. When the subway first opened, there were just 9 miles (14.48 km) of track. A hundred years later, this figure had soared to 842 miles (1,355 km), 660

According to the MTA's Web site (http://www.mta.info):

The Arts for Transit commissions public art that is seen by hundreds of thousands of city-dwellers as well as national and international visitors who use the subway and rail system. As the MTA rehabilitates subway and commuter rail stations through its Capital Program, it uses a portion of the funds to install permanent works of art. . . . Both well-established and emerging artists add to a growing collection of works created in the materials of the system—mosaic, ceramic, tile, bronze, steel, and faceted glass. The art can be seen in the miles of walls within the system and in the gates, windscreens, plazas, and architecture.

The creation of what is regarded by some as the world's largest art museum in the subway of New York is appropriate, given that art in transit was written into the original construction contract. According to the contract, "Great public work worthy of attractive design, even beauty" was to commence. Happily, this art as part of transit tradition continues into the twenty-first century.

(1062 km) of which were in current use. There were now 468 stations, 277 of them underground. In 2004, 4.5 million passengers rode the subway's 230 route miles (370 km) every day, a total of 1.3 billion people per year.

The only statistics that weren't climbing, and were in fact declining, were crime related. In 1990, 17,000 serious felonies were reported in the subway system. By 2004, the number had fallen to 2,700. The police department's Transit Bureau chief called the decline "pretty amazing."

Yet, all was not idyllic in the subway's centennial year. On September 8, 2004, a downpour immobilized much of the subway system, highlighting, as Ian Urbina wrote in the *New York Times*, "how an otherwise durable transit network still finds itself particularly vulnerable to an altogether predictable threat: a quick, heavy rain." Hundreds of thousands of commuters were stranded as the subway's 720 sump pumps worked frantically to relieve the system of millions of gallons of water. "No subway system in the world is designed to handle that kind of storm flow," Robert E. Paaswell, former director of the Chicago Transit Authority, told the *Times*. "And if the above-ground storm system gets overloaded, then you're going to have double the problems underground."

In 2007, it happened again. This author, making his way from Lincoln Center to West 34th Street, descended into the subway station at Columbus Circle to find railcars packed with people creeping along the old IRT line. There would be no subway rides that day, as commuters jammed buses and flagged hundreds of yellow taxies in a desperate attempt to move about Manhattan.

Although flooding, it seemed, would always be a New York Subway problem, relief for commuters was on the way when, in 2007, plans were once again put into effect for construction of the long-delayed Second Avenue Subway Project. No one could deny that the East Side needed transit relief. Since its two els came down, one in 1942 and the other in 1956, the area has been serviced by only one mass-transit route—the Lexington Avenue line (trains 4, 5, and 6). Proposals to build an additional East Side subway date back to 1929; actual construction of several tunnel segments did not take place until the early 1970s. Construction was suspended soon after, however, when funds dried up.

By 2007, New York was enjoying its first new subway construction in more than 50 years. Digging on the 8.5-mile (13.67 km) Second Avenue line had begun again, at a cost of more than $1 billion per mile. The subway system that united and, in no small way, built the New York known to millions is still expanding, growing, and defining the Big Apple. The New York Subway is forever being reborn, experiencing a technical and cultural renaissance.

1898 Greater New York City is formed.

1900 *March 24* Construction of the IRT subway begins.

1903 *October 24* Ten workers are killed in the Fort George Tunnel explosion.

1904 *October 27* The official opening and dedication of the first nine miles of IRT subway is held.

1908 *August 1* The IRT subway project is completed.

1913 *March 19* New York's Public Service Commission issues Dual Contracts to the IRT and the BRT.

1918 *November 1* The Malbone Street Wreck kills 93 people.

TIMELINE

1900
March 24 Construction of the IRT subway begins.

1908
August 1 The IRT subway project is completed.

1900 ——— 1923

1903
October 24 Ten workers are killed in the Fort George Tunnel explosion.

1904
October 27 The official opening and dedication of the first nine miles of IRT subway is held.

1923
June The Brooklyn-Manhattan Transit Company (BMT) is formed after acquiring assets of the BRT.

1919 *January 1* The BRT goes into receivership.

1921 *January* Edward Luciano and five BRT officials are acquitted in the Malbone Street Wreck.

1923 *June* The Brooklyn-Manhattan Transit Company (BMT) is formed after acquiring assets of the BRT.

Yankee Stadium, built next to the IRT line in the Bronx, opens for play.

1925 New Yorkers average 276 subway rides per year.

March 14 Construction begins on the new, municipally owned Independent Subway System (IND).

1925
March 14 Construction begins on the new, municipally owned Independent Subway System (IND).

1939
December 12 Subway unification (IRT, BMT, IND) marks the largest railroad merger in U.S. history.

1984
December 22 Bernard Goetz shoots four young men he says were threatening him on the subway.

1925 ✖✖✖✖✖✖✖✖✖✖✖✖✖✖✖✖✖✖ **2007**

1932
September 10 The first IND route opens.

January 1 The Transport Workers Union (TWU) calls its first strike, shutting down the New York Subway system for 12 days.

1966

2007
Construction on the 8.5-mile Second Avenue Subway line begins again.

1932   The IRT goes into receivership.

September 10   The first IND route opens.

1934   *January 1*   Fiorello H. LaGuardia becomes mayor of New York.

1939   *December 12*   Subway unification (IRT, BMT, IND) marks the largest railroad merger in U.S. history.

1940   *December 14*   The last IND route opens.

1946   *December 23*   An all-time daily record for subway passengers is set at 8,872,244.

1948   *July 1*   Subway fare rises from a nickel to a dime.

1966   *January 1*   The Transport Workers Union (TWU) calls its first strike, shutting down the New York Subway system for 12 days.

1970   Extensive graffiti first appears on subway cars and subway trains.

1980   *April 1*   The TWU calls its second subway strike, shutting down the New York Subway system for 11 days.

1981   The MTA receives $8.1 billion in funding to upgrade the New York Subway system.

1984   David Gunn takes over as president of the Transit Authority (TA) and begins the Clean Car graffiti cleanup campaign.

December 22   Bernard Goetz shoots four young men he says were threatening him on the subway.

1989   The New York Subway is declared graffiti-free.

2004   The New York Subway system celebrates its centennial.

2005   *December 20*   The TWU strikes for the third time, shutting down the New York Subway system for three days.

2007   *August 8*   The New York Subway floods, stranding thousands of passengers.

Construction on the 8.5-mile (13.6) Second Avenue Subway line begins again.

GLOSSARY

borough   One of the five political divisions of New York City.

conduit   A natural or artificial channel through which something is conducted.

cut and cover   A construction method whereby a rectangular hole is dug in the ground from service level.

dray   A vehicle, usually without sides, used to haul goods.

entrepreneur   One who is of a business mind; able to organize a business enterprise.

girder   A large principal beam designed to support concentrated loads at isolated points along its length.

graffiti   Unauthorized writing or drawing on a public surface.

guillotine   A shearing machine or instrument (such as a paper cutter) that, in action, resembles a guillotine.

magistrate   An official entrusted with the administration of the law.

mastodon   An extinct mammal, related to the mammoth.

motorman   One who drives a train, usually a subway.

motor switchman   One who drives a train, usually a subway, in the field yard (not carrying passengers).

municipal   Government ownership.

omnibus   A public vehicle designed to carry a large number of passengers.

panhandling   Stopping someone on the street and ask for food or money.

pneumatic   Describes a device that is moved or worked by air pressure.

portal   The approach or entrance to a bridge or tunnel.

post-and-lintel   Wall construction using a framework of vertical posts and horizontal beams to carry floor and roof loads.

privy   An outhouse; a place to relieve oneself.

ranger   A support beam.

rectify   To change alternating current into direct current.

route miles   Actual subway miles (as opposed to track miles, which could be more).

scratchitti   A form of graffiti that is made by etching and carving one's tag on an object instead of using tools like marker ink or spray paint.

siding   A short railroad track connected to a main track.

sinking fund   A fund set up and accumulated by regular deposits for paying off the principal of a debt when it falls due.

Tammany Hall   A nineteenth-century political organization in New York City known for extensive corruption.

terra cotta   A hard, fired clay that is reddish-brown in color when unglazed; used for architectural facings and ornaments, tile units, and pottery.

vertigo   A sensation of motion in which the individual's surroundings seem to spin dizzily.

viaduct   A long, elevated roadway that usually consists of a series of short spans supported on arches, piers, or columns.

vigilante   A member of a volunteer committee organized to suppress and punish crime.

BIBLIOGRAPHY

Ascher, Kate. *The Works: Anatomy of a City.* New York: Penguin, 2005.

Barnard, Anne. "Subway to Bring 2nd Ave. Closer, but Some Neighbors Will Miss the Distance." *New York Times*, October 7, 2007. http://www.nytimes.com/2007/10/07/nyregion/07subway.html.

Barron, James. "Subway to Rooftops, a Storm Brings Havoc to New York." *New York Times*, August 9, 2007.

"BMT Sea Beach N Line." Available online: http://www.rapidtransit.net/net/faq/nyc/seabeach.html.

Brooks, Michael. *Subway City: Riding the Trains, Reading New York.* New Brunswick, N.J.: Rutgers University Press, 1997.

Ching, Francis. *A Visual Dictionary of Architecture.* New York: John Wiley & Sons, 1995.

Conklin, Croff. *All About Subways.* New York: J. Messner, 1938.

ConstructionCompany.com. "Historic Construction Company Project—New York City Subway System." Available online: http://www.constructioncompany.com/historic-construction-projects/new-york-city-subway/.

Cudahy, Brian. *Under the Sidewalks of New York: The Story of the Greatest Subway System in the World.* New York: Fordham University Press, 1995.

Cudahy, Brian. *The Malbone Street Wreck.* New York: Fordham University Press, 1999.

Diehl, Lorraine. *Subways: The Tracks That Built New York City.* New York: Clarkson Potter, 2004.

Dwyer, Jim. *Subway Lives: 24 Hours in the Life of the New York City Subway.* New York: Crown, 1991.

Eliot, Marc. *Down 42nd Street: Sex, Money, Culture, and Politics at the Crossroads of the World.* New York: Rebel Road, 2001.

Fischler, Stan. *The Subway and the City: Celebrating a Century.* New York: Frank Merriwell, 2004.

Hill, Laban. *Harlem Stomp: A Cultural History of the Harlem Renaissance.* New York: Little Brown, 2003.

Hood, Clifton. *722 Miles: The Building of the Subways and How They Transformed New York.* Baltimore: The John Hopkins University Press, 2004.

Lavis, Fred. *Building the New Rapid Transit System of New York City.* Belleville, N.J.: Xplorer Press, 1996.

Mass Transit magazine. Available online: www.masstransit-mag.com.

Michaels, Kerry, and Stuart Math. *River of Steel: The Building of the New York City Subway.* DVD. New York: Stuart Math Films, 1994.

New York City Subway. Available online: http://nycsubway.org.

"New York City Subway." Wikipedia. Available online: http://en.wikipedia.org/wiki/New_York_City_Subway.

"New York Subway Map 1972." Available online: http://www.visualcomplexity.com/vc/project_details.cfm?index=266&id=266&domain.

New York Times. "A Ride on the Elevated." August 1, 1880. http://query.nytimes.com/mem/archive-free/pdf?res-990DE3DEI53BE033A25752C0A96E9C94619FD7CF

New York Times. "Hold 3 Employees for B.R.T. Wreck; 89 Dead, 103 Hurt." November 3, 1918. http://query.nytimes.com/mem/archive-free/pdf?res-9E04E4DF1239E13ABC4B53DFB7678383609EDE

New York Times. "Interesting Facts About Our Subway." October 28, 1904. http://query.nytimes.com/mem/archive-free/pdf?res-9F00EFD7I230EE32A2575BC2A9669D946597D6CF

New York Times. "Man Killed in Subway." November 4, 1904. http://query.nytimes.com/mem/archive-free/pdf?res-9500E1D8113DE633A25757C0A9679D946597D6CF

New York Times. "Our Subway Open, 150,000 Try It. October 28, 1904. http://query.nytimes.com/mem/archive-free/pdf?res-9E06EFD7I230EE32A2575BC2A9669D946597D6CF

New York Times. "Relief of Broadway and the People of New York—An Underground Railroad Necessity." December 22,

1865. http://query.nytimes.com/mem/archive-free/pdf?res-
9E0CE2D6153BE637A2575IC2A9649D94691D7CF

New York Times. "River Breaks in on Belmont Tube." July 3,
1906. http://query.nytimes.com/mem/archive-free/pdf?res-
9905EEDA1E3EE733A25750C0A9619C946797D6CF

New York Times. "Rush-Hour Blockade Jams Subway Crowds."
October 28, 1904. http://query.nytimes.com/mem/archive-free/
pdf?res-950IEFDFI63DE733A2575AC2A9669D946597D6CF

New York Times. "Scores Killed or Maimed in Brighton
Tunnel Wreck." November 2, 1918. http://query.
nytimes.com/mem/archive-free/pdf?res-
9FO4EED6I539EI3ABC4A53DFB76783836O9EDE

New York Times. "Some Lines Hit Hard by Subway
Competition." October 29, 1904. http://query.
nytimes.com/mem/archive-free/pdf?res-
9BO5EEDFI63DE733A2575AC2A9669D946597D6CF

New York Times. "Subway Air." November 11, 1904. http://query.
nytimes.com/mem/archive-free/pdf?res-
9FO4E6D6I23OEE32A25753CIA9679D946597D6CF

New York Times. "Subway Station Advertising." November 3,
1904. http://query.nytimes.com/mem/archive-free/pdf?res-
9CO6E2DDII3BE63IA2575OCOA9679D946597D6CF

New York Times. "Traffic Jam Relief." November 18, 1921.
http://query.nytimes.com/mem/archive-free/pdf?res-
99O4E7DEII3CE533A2575BCIA9679D946O95D6CF

New York Times. "Tunnel Company Is Incorporated."
February 20, 1900. http://query.nytimes.com/mem/
archive-free/pdf?res-9EOIEODBI438BE43OA75753C2A9649
C946I97D6CF

New York Times. "Women Faint in Bad Subway
Atmosphere." November 6, 1904. http://query.
nytimes.com/mem/archive-free/pdf?res-
9BOIEFDEI23BE733A25755COA9679D946597D6CF

New York Transit Museum. *Subway Style: 100 Years of Architecture & Design in the New York City Subway.* New York:
Stewart, Tabori & Chang, 2004.

New York Transit Museum, and Vivian Heller. *The City Beneath Us: Building the New York Subways*. New York: W.W. Norton & Company, 2004.

O'Connor, Anahad, and Graham Bowley. "Tornado Hits Brooklyn; Subway Back in Service." *New York Times*, August 8, 2007. Available online: http://www.nytimes.com/2007/08/08/nyregion/08cnd-weather.html?hp.

Purrington, Ginna. "Robert Moses: A Tribute to the Man and His Impact on the Borough." *Queens Gazette*, June 30, 1999.

Stacey, Michelle. *The Fasting Girl: A True Victorian Medical Mystery*. New York: Penguin, 2002.

"Subway Centennia." Metropolitan Transit Authority. Available online: http://www.mta.info/mta/centennial.htm.

Transportation Workers Union Local 100. Available online: http://www.twulocal100.org.

Urbina, Ian. "Aging Sewers Are Unable to Keep Up With the Flow." *New York Times*, September 9, 2004. Available online: htp//www.nytimes.com/2004/09/09/nyregion/09water.html

Wilson, Tracy V. "How Subways Work." HowStuffWorks. Available online: http://travel.howstuffworks.com/subway.htm.

FURTHER RESOURCES

Brimner, Larry. *Subway: The Story of Tunnels, Tubes, and Tracks*. Honesdale, Pa.: Boyds Mills Press, Inc. 2004.

DuBois Jacobs, Paul, Jennifer Swender, and Selina Alko. *My Subway Ride*. Layton, Utah: Gibbs Smith, 2004.

McNeese, Tim. *The New York Subway System*. San Diego: Lucent, 1997.

New York Transit Museum. *New York Subway Trains: 12 Classic Punch and Build Trains*. New York: New York Transit Museum, 2004.

Weitzman, David. *A Subway for New York*. New York: Farrar, Straus and Giroux, 2005.

WEB SITES

Forgotten Subways and Trains
http://www.forgotten-ny.com/SUBWAYS/Subways%20homepage/subways.html

History of Subway Graffiti
http://durocia.com/new%20duro%20site/subway_history.htm

New York Transit Museum
http://www.mta.info/mta/museum/

PICTURE CREDITS

ABOUT THE AUTHOR

RONALD A. REIS is the author of 18 books, including young adult biographies of Lou Gehrig and Jonas Salk, and stories of the Dust Bowl and the Empire State Building. He is the chairperson of the technology department at Los Angeles Valley College.